Cracking the Talent Acquisition (Recruiter) Interview: 100 Top Questions & Answer

With each chapter dedicated to a specific topic, "Cracking the Talent Acquisition (Recruiter) Interview: 100 Top Questions & Answer" is your comprehensive companion to conquering the multifaceted challenges of talent acquisition. Whether you are a seasoned recruiter seeking to enhance your skills or a candidate preparing for diverse scenarios, this guide is your definitive resource for success in talent acquisition interviews.

However, the author and publisher disclaim any liability for any loss or risk that may be incurred as a consequence of the use and application of the contents of this book.

Cover design by Eva Mariam.

Don't walk-in to your next interview without reading this treasure book!

Embark on an enriching journey into the realm of talent acquisition with "Cracking the Talent Acquisition (Recruiter) Interview: 100 Top Questions & Answer" As a seasoned recruiter, you understand the intricacies of the recruitment process, and this book is meticulously crafted to empower both recruiters and talent job seekers in mastering the art of interviews across diverse topics.

Unveil the secrets of effective recruitment strategy and planning, explore advanced techniques in candidate sourcing and outreach, and sharpen your skills in candidate screening and assessment. Navigate through the nuances of interviewing and selection, while gaining valuable insights into the critical aspects of employer branding, talent pipelines, and networking.

With dedicated chapters on collaboration with hiring managers, data-driven recruiting, and fostering diversity and inclusion, this book ensures a holistic understanding of contemporary recruitment practices. Dive into the latest trends in talent acquisition technology, explore the intricacies of candidate experience, and unravel the complexities of legal and compliance aspects.

Adaptability and resilience are key in the ever-evolving recruitment landscape, and this book provides invaluable guidance on overcoming challenges and continuous learning. From scenario-based questions to effective collaboration with HR and hiring teams, each chapter is a treasure trove of knowledge.

Whether you're addressing the nuances of remote and hybrid hiring, prioritizing time management, or embracing leadership and mentorship, this guide equips you with practical strategies. Discover the significance of global talent acquisition, explore metrics and reporting techniques, and understand the integration of HR technology in shaping a successful talent acquisition journey.

Engage with real-world scenarios and refine your approach through feedback and improvement strategies. Uncover the power of employment brand and employee referrals, and learn the art of leadership and mentorship in talent acquisition. Continuous learning and professional development are at the core of this guide, ensuring that you stay ahead in the dynamic field of talent acquisition.

Table of Contents

Recruitment Strategy and Planning

A recruitment strategy is a plan of action that an organization uses to find, attract, and hire qualified candidates for a specific role or set of roles.

Recruitment planning involves identifying the hiring needs of the organization, defining job requirements, and developing a plan to attract and select the best candidates.

Here are some key steps in recruitment strategy and planning for a Talent Acquisition Specialist specializing in top-tier IT companies:

1. Understand the hiring needs: Begin by understanding the specific hiring needs of the organization. This includes determining the roles and skills required, as well as the timeline for hiring.

2. Define job requirements: Clearly define the job requirements, including the qualifications, experience, and skills needed for the role. This will help in creating targeted job descriptions and screening candidates effectively.

3. Develop a sourcing strategy: Identify the most effective channels for sourcing candidates. This could include job boards, social media platforms, industry-specific websites, and professional networks. Consider both active and passive candidate sourcing strategies.

4. Create compelling job descriptions: Craft job descriptions that accurately depict the role, responsibilities, and qualifications required. Use clear and concise language, highlighting the unique aspects of the position and the company culture.

5. Build a talent pipeline: Proactively build a talent pipeline by engaging with potential candidates through networking events, career fairs, and industry conferences. Maintain relationships with top candidates even if there are no immediate openings.

6. Utilize technology: Leverage technology tools such as applicant tracking systems (ATS) and recruitment software to streamline the hiring process. These tools can help in managing candidate data, automating workflows, and improving collaboration between hiring team members.

7. Implement an effective screening process: Develop a screening process that efficiently filters out unqualified candidates and identifies the most suitable candidates for further evaluation. This could involve resume screening, phone interviews, technical assessments, and behavioral interviews.

8. Assess cultural fit: In addition to assessing technical skills, evaluate cultural fit during the recruitment process. This can be done through behavioral-based interview questions and assessing alignment with the organization's values and work culture.

9. Evaluate and select candidates: Conduct thorough evaluations of shortlisted candidates, considering their qualifications, skills, experience, cultural fit, and potential for growth within the organization. Involve relevant stakeholders in the decision-making process.

10. Develop an onboarding plan: Once candidates are selected, develop an onboarding plan to ensure a smooth transition into the organization. This includes providing necessary training, assigning mentors, and setting clear expectations.

Real-world example:

For example, a Talent Acquisition Specialist specializing in top-tier IT companies may develop a recruitment strategy and plan for hiring software developers. The strategy may involve sourcing candidates through dedicated developer communities, conducting technical assessments, and assessing cultural fit within a fast-paced, innovative work environment.

How do you develop a recruitment strategy for hard-to-fill positions?

Answer

Developing a recruitment strategy for hard-to-fill positions requires a targeted and proactive approach. Here are the steps to follow:

1. Understand the position: Start by thoroughly understanding the requirements and responsibilities of the hard-to-fill position. This includes understanding the technical skills, experience level, and any specific qualifications or certifications needed.

2. Identify your target audience: Research and identify the specific groups or communities where potential candidates with the required skills and qualifications are likely to be active. This could include online forums, industry events, or professional networking platforms.

3. Build a strong employer brand: Highlight your company's unique selling points and competitive advantages to attract top talent.

Showcase your company culture, employee benefits, and success stories to create a positive image that appeals to potential candidates.

4. Craft compelling job descriptions: Clearly communicate the role, responsibilities, and expectations in the job description. Highlight the unique aspects of the position and emphasize the opportunities for growth and development.

5. Utilize targeted sourcing strategies: Use a combination of traditional and innovative sourcing methods to reach the desired audience. This could include leveraging social media platforms, attending industry-specific events, partnering with specialized recruitment agencies, or utilizing employee referrals.

6. Engage passive candidates: Hard-to-fill positions often require reaching out to passive candidates who may not be actively looking for a job. Develop personalized outreach strategies to engage with these candidates and showcase the value of the opportunity.

7. Streamline the selection process: Simplify and streamline the application and interview process to avoid losing candidates due to lengthy or complicated procedures. This includes setting clear expectations, providing timely feedback, and being responsive to candidate inquiries.

8. Offer competitive compensation and benefits: To attract top talent for hard-to-fill positions, it is essential to offer competitive compensation packages and attractive benefits. Research industry standards and ensure your offers are in line with market expectations.

9. Provide a positive candidate experience: Ensure that candidates have a positive experience throughout the recruitment process, regardless of the outcome. This includes clear and timely communication, respectful interactions, and providing feedback whenever possible.

10. Continuously evaluate and improve: Regularly review the effectiveness of your recruitment strategy and make adjustments as needed. Analyze the success rate of different sourcing methods, track time-to-hire metrics, and gather feedback from candidates and hiring managers for continuous improvement.

Discuss your experience with workforce planning?

Answer

I have extensive experience with workforce planning as a Talent Acquisition Specialist specializing in top-tier IT companies.

Workforce planning involves analyzing an organization's current and future workforce needs and developing strategies to address those needs.

One example of my experience with workforce planning is when I worked with a top-tier IT company to develop a plan for hiring software engineers.

I conducted a thorough analysis of the company's current software engineering team and identified areas where additional resources were needed.

Based on this analysis, I worked with hiring managers to develop a hiring plan that included specific goals for the number of software engineers to be hired and a timeline for the hiring process.

I also worked closely with the HR team to develop strategies for attracting top talent, including creating job descriptions that highlighted the company's unique culture and benefits.

Throughout the hiring process, I regularly reviewed and adjusted the workforce plan based on changes in the company's needs and market conditions.

How do you prioritize and plan for multiple open positions simultaneously?

Answer

1. Assess the urgency and criticality of each open position: Evaluate the impact that each position has on the overall goals and objectives of the organization. Determine which positions are more time-sensitive or have a higher impact on the success of the company. For example, if there is an immediate need for a crucial role that directly affects the productivity of the team, it should be given higher priority over other positions that may not have an immediate impact.

2. Create a timeline and set deadlines: Develop a clear timeline for each open position, including key milestones and deadlines. It is essential to establish realistic expectations and communicate them

with the hiring team and stakeholders. This will help in managing expectations and ensuring that the recruitment process stays on track. For instance, setting a deadline for shortlisting candidates, conducting interviews, and making a final decision can help in managing multiple positions simultaneously.

3. Allocate resources and prioritize tasks: Determine the resources required for each position, such as budget, sourcing channels, and interview panel. Allocate resources based on the urgency and importance of the position. Prioritize tasks accordingly, such as sourcing, screening, and interviewing candidates. For instance, if there is a shortage of resources, it might be necessary to focus on positions that require immediate attention and delay others that can afford more time.

4. Use technology and automation: Leverage technology and automation tools to streamline the recruitment process. Applicant tracking systems can help in managing multiple positions simultaneously by automating tasks such as resume screening, scheduling interviews, and tracking candidate progress. These tools can save time and ensure a more efficient hiring process.

5. Regularly communicate and provide updates: Maintain open and transparent communication with the hiring team, stakeholders, and candidates. Provide regular updates on the progress of each position, including challenges faced and potential delays. This will help in managing expectations and keeping everyone informed about the status of the recruitment process.

6. Monitor and adjust the plan: Continuously monitor the progress of each open position and make adjustments to the plan if needed. Regularly review the timeline, resource allocation, and overall recruitment strategy. If any position is facing unforeseen delays or challenges, consider reallocating resources or revising the timeline to ensure that all positions are given proper attention and are filled within the desired timeframe.

What methods do you use to forecast future hiring needs?

Answer

Conducting a thorough analysis of current workforce and future business objectives

Reviewing historical data on employee turnover rates, growth patterns, and industry trends

Collaborating with department heads and executives to understand their future staffing needs

Monitoring market conditions and industry developments that may impact talent availability

Utilizing predictive analytics and workforce planning tools to project future hiring needs

Engaging in talent pipeline development and succession planning to identify internal candidates for future roles

Leveraging external resources such as industry reports, job market data, and competitor analysis to inform hiring forecasts

Regularly reviewing and updating hiring plans based on changing business conditions and priorities

Sourcing and Candidate Outreach

Sourcing and candidate outreach are crucial aspects of the talent acquisition process for a talent acquisition specialist specializing in top-tier IT companies. These activities involve identifying potential candidates and reaching out to them to gauge their interest in job opportunities. Here are some key points to consider:

• Sourcing involves actively searching for candidates who possess the desired skills and qualifications for the job. This can be done through various channels such as job boards, social media platforms, professional networking websites, and industry-specific forums. The goal is to cast a wide net to attract a diverse pool of potential candidates.

• Candidate outreach is the process of contacting potential candidates and engaging them in conversations about job opportunities. This can be done through email, phone calls, or social media messages. It is important to personalize these outreach efforts and tailor them to the individual candidate's interests and motivations. Real-world example: A talent acquisition specialist specializing in top-tier IT companies might use LinkedIn, a professional networking platform, to source and reach out to potential candidates. They could search for individuals with specific skills and experience, and then send them personalized messages expressing interest in their qualifications and inviting them to apply for open positions.

• Hands-on exercise: Conduct a search on a job board or professional networking website for candidates with specific skills and qualifications. Identify potential candidates and draft a sample outreach message to engage them in a conversation about job opportunities.

• Visual aids: Consider creating a visual diagram to illustrate the sourcing and candidate outreach process. This could include steps such as identifying target candidate profiles, searching for potential candidates, reaching out to them, and tracking their responses.

• Engaging formatting: Use bullet points, headings, and subheadings to organize information and make it easy for readers to navigate. Include relevant examples and case studies to illustrate key points and make the content more engaging.

• Logical progression: Present the information in a logical order, starting with an overview of sourcing and candidate outreach, then diving into specific strategies and tactics. Make sure each point flows smoothly into the next and supports the overall objective of attracting top-tier IT candidates.

• Clear objectives: Clearly state the objectives of sourcing and candidate outreach, which are to identify potential candidates with the desired skills and qualifications and engage them in conversations about job opportunities. Emphasize the importance of personalization and tailoring outreach efforts to individual candidates.

How do you identify and attract passive candidates?

Answer

Identifying passive candidates:

• Utilize professional networking platforms like LinkedIn to search for professionals who are currently employed in top-tier IT companies.

• Look for professionals who have relevant skills and experience in the IT industry.

• Pay attention to individuals who are highly sought after and have a track record of success in their current roles.

• Monitor industry events, conferences, and online forums to identify professionals who are actively participating and contributing to discussions.

Attracting passive candidates:

• Highlight the unique opportunities and benefits that your organization can offer.

• Showcase the company's culture, work-life balance, and career growth opportunities.

• Share success stories and testimonials from current employees to demonstrate the positive experiences of working at your company.

• Provide information about the specific projects and technologies that candidates would be working on, emphasizing the cutting-edge nature of the work.

• Offer competitive compensation packages, including salary, bonuses, and benefits.

• Engage with passive candidates through personalized messages and invitations to connect, showing genuine interest in their background and skills.

• Utilize employee referrals to tap into the networks of current employees.

• Use targeted advertising on professional networking platforms to reach passive candidates.

Example: When identifying passive candidates, a talent acquisition specialist might search for professionals on LinkedIn who have experience working as software engineers in top-tier IT companies. They would look for individuals who have a strong track record of success and are currently employed in roles that require similar skills. When attracting passive candidates, the specialist would highlight the cutting-edge projects and technologies that the candidates would have the opportunity to work on, as well as the competitive compensation packages offered by the organization.

Can you describe a successful sourcing campaign you've led?

Answer

Yes, I can describe a successful sourcing campaign I've led. Here are the details:

Objective: The objective of the sourcing campaign was to attract top-tier IT talent for a leading technology company.

Target Audience: The target audience for this campaign was experienced IT professionals with expertise in specific programming languages and technologies.

Sourcing Channels: I utilized a combination of online job boards, professional networking platforms, and industry-specific forums to reach out to potential candidates.

Messaging: The messaging in the campaign focused on highlighting the exciting projects and opportunities available at the company, as well as the competitive compensation and benefits package.

Engagement: I actively engaged with potential candidates through personalized messages and emails, showcasing the company's culture and values.

Screening and Evaluation: I carefully screened and evaluated the resumes and profiles of interested candidates, shortlisting those who met the desired criteria.

Interview Process: I coordinated and scheduled interviews with the shortlisted candidates, ensuring a smooth and efficient process.

Offer Negotiation: I worked closely with the HR team to negotiate competitive offers with the selected candidates, taking into consideration their skills, experience, and market trends.

Successful Hires: As a result of the sourcing campaign, we were able to successfully hire several top-tier IT professionals who made significant contributions to the company's projects and growth.

What tools and platforms do you use for candidate outreach?

Answer

As a Talent Acquisition Specialist specializing in top-tier IT companies, I utilize a variety of tools and platforms for candidate outreach. These include:

• LinkedIn: I leverage LinkedIn's extensive network of professionals to identify and connect with potential candidates. I use advanced search filters to narrow down the pool of candidates based on specific skills, experience, and location. I also utilize LinkedIn messaging and InMail to reach out to candidates directly.

• Job boards: I post job listings on popular job boards such as Indeed, Glassdoor, and Dice to attract candidates who are actively searching for new opportunities. These platforms allow me to reach a large audience and receive applications from interested candidates.

• Social media: I utilize social media platforms like Twitter, Facebook, and Instagram to promote job openings and engage with potential candidates. I create visually appealing posts with relevant hashtags and encourage sharing to increase exposure.

• Employee referral programs: I leverage the existing network of employees within the organization to source potential candidates. I encourage employees to refer qualified individuals for open positions and provide incentives for successful referrals.

• Talent acquisition software: I utilize applicant tracking systems (ATS) and candidate relationship management (CRM) tools to streamline the candidate outreach process. These tools allow me to track and manage candidate applications, schedule interviews, and communicate with candidates efficiently.

By utilizing these tools and platforms, I can effectively reach out to a wide range of candidates and attract top talent for top-tier IT companies.

How do you ensure a diverse candidate pool?

Answer

Implement a diverse sourcing strategy by utilizing various channels to reach candidates from different backgrounds and demographics. This can include job boards, social media platforms, professional networking sites, diversity-focused organizations, and employee referrals.

Review and update job descriptions and requirements to remove any unnecessary or biased criteria that may limit the candidate pool. Use inclusive language and focus on the essential skills and qualifications needed for the role.

Engage in targeted outreach efforts to underrepresented groups in the industry. This can involve attending diversity-focused career fairs, partnering with organizations that support minority candidates, or sponsoring events that promote diversity and inclusion.

Ensure the selection process is fair and unbiased by implementing standardized interview questions and evaluation criteria. Train hiring managers on unconscious bias and provide guidelines for assessing candidates based on their skills and potential rather than personal characteristics.

Create a welcoming and inclusive company culture that values diversity. Showcase the diversity of your existing employees in your recruitment materials and highlight the company's commitment to diversity and inclusion.

Monitor and analyze recruitment data to track the effectiveness of diversity initiatives. Identify any gaps or areas for improvement and adjust strategies accordingly.

Provide unconscious bias training for the entire hiring team to raise awareness and ensure fair evaluation of candidates.

Establish partnerships with diversity-focused organizations, such as professional associations or educational institutions, to tap into their networks and access a wider pool of diverse candidates.

Candidate Screening and Assessment

Screening and assessing candidates is a crucial step in the talent acquisition process, especially when it comes to hiring top-tier IT professionals. It involves evaluating candidates' qualifications, skills, and overall fit for the role and the company. Here are some key points to consider when screening and assessing candidates for a Talent Acquisition Specialist role in top-tier IT companies:

1. Reviewing resumes and applications: Start by reviewing resumes and applications to identify candidates who meet the basic qualifications and requirements for the role. Look for relevant experience, skills, certifications, and education. Pay attention to any red flags or gaps in employment history.

2. Conducting phone interviews: Phone interviews are a great way to assess candidates' communication skills, professionalism, and initial fit for the role. Prepare a set of standardized questions to ask each candidate and take notes on their responses. Focus on their experience in talent acquisition, IT industry knowledge, and their ability to work with top-tier professionals.

3. Administering skills assessments: Depending on the specific role and requirements, consider administering skills assessments to evaluate candidates' technical abilities. This could include coding challenges, problem-solving exercises, or tests to assess their knowledge of specific programming languages or technologies. These assessments can help you gauge candidates' level of expertise and suitability for the role.

4. Conducting in-person or virtual interviews: Once you have narrowed down the pool of candidates, schedule in-person or virtual interviews to further assess their fit for the role and the company culture. Prepare a mix of behavioral and technical questions to evaluate their skills, experience, and problem-solving abilities. Use real-world scenarios or case studies to see how candidates approach and solve complex problems.

5. Checking references and conducting background checks: Before making a final decision, it's important to check candidates' references and conduct background checks to verify their employment history, qualifications, and any potential red flags. This step can help you validate the information provided by candidates and ensure you are making an informed hiring decision.

Real-world example: Let's say you are hiring a Talent Acquisition Specialist for a top-tier IT company. You receive numerous resumes and applications, and you start by reviewing them to identify candidates who meet the basic qualifications, such as a bachelor's degree in HR or a related field, a minimum of 3 years of experience in talent acquisition, and proficiency in IT industry terminology. You then conduct phone interviews with the selected candidates, asking questions about their experience in recruiting top-tier IT professionals, their familiarity with emerging technologies, and their ability to handle high-volume hiring. Based on their responses, you shortlist a few candidates and administer skills assessments to evaluate their technical capabilities. Finally, you conduct in-person interviews with the top candidates, asking them to solve real-world recruiting challenges and assessing their cultural fit for the company.

Summarized answer: Screening and assessing candidates for a Talent Acquisition Specialist role in top-tier IT companies involves reviewing resumes, conducting phone interviews, administering skills assessments, conducting in-person interviews, and checking references. It is important to evaluate candidates' qualifications, skills, and overall fit for the role and the company. Real-world examples and hands-on assessments can help in making informed hiring decisions.

What criteria do you use to screen resumes effectively?

Answer
When screening resumes for talent acquisition in top-tier IT companies, I use the following criteria:
• Relevant experience: I look for candidates who have previous experience in similar roles or industries. This ensures they have the necessary skills and knowledge to excel in the position.
• Technical skills: IT roles require specific technical skills, so I evaluate resumes for the presence of relevant programming languages, software applications, and certifications.
• Education: While not always a determining factor, a strong educational background can indicate a candidate's ability to learn

and adapt quickly. I consider degrees, diplomas, and certifications in relevant fields.

• Job stability: I pay attention to the candidate's employment history, looking for patterns of job-hopping or long-term commitment. This helps me assess their reliability and dedication.

• Achievements and projects: I look for candidates who have achieved notable milestones or worked on impactful projects. This demonstrates their ability to contribute effectively to the organization.

• Clear and concise formatting: Resumes that are well-organized, easy to read, and free of errors are more likely to catch my attention. I look for clear headings, bullet points, and consistent formatting.

• Keywords and phrases: I scan resumes for keywords and phrases that are relevant to the position or industry. This helps me quickly identify candidates who have the desired skills and experience.

• Attention to detail: Attention to detail is crucial in IT roles, so I pay attention to the candidate's resume for any typos, grammatical errors, or inconsistencies.

• Cultural fit: I consider whether the candidate's values, work style, and personality align with the company culture. This helps me assess their potential fit within the organization.

Discuss your approach to initial candidate assessments?

Answer

During the initial candidate assessment process, my approach focuses on evaluating the qualifications, skills, and experience of the candidates to determine their suitability for the position. Here is an overview of my approach:

I begin by thoroughly reviewing the candidate's resume and application materials to understand their educational background, work experience, and relevant skills. This helps me to quickly gauge if the candidate meets the basic requirements for the role.

Next, I conduct a preliminary phone screening to assess the candidate's communication skills, professionalism, and interest in the position. I ask specific questions related to their experience and qualifications to gather more information and evaluate their fit for the role.

If the candidate successfully passes the phone screening, I schedule an initial in-person or video interview. This interview is focused on assessing the candidate's technical skills and domain knowledge. I ask open-ended questions and present real-world scenarios to understand how the candidate approaches problem-solving and critical thinking.

Additionally, I may request the candidate to complete a skills assessment or technical test to further evaluate their abilities. This can be done in-person or online, depending on the nature of the role.

After the initial interview and assessments, I carefully review all the gathered information and compare it against the job requirements and the company's culture. This helps me to determine if the candidate is a good fit for the position and the organization.

Finally, I provide feedback to the hiring manager or team and recommend the most suitable candidates for further consideration in the hiring process.

I believe that a well-structured and thorough initial candidate assessment process is crucial in identifying top talent and ensuring a successful hiring outcome.

How do you determine if a candidate is the right cultural fit for the organization?

Answer

Conduct behavioral interviews: Ask candidates about their past work experiences and how they handled specific situations to gauge their cultural fit. Look for examples of teamwork, problem-solving, and adaptability.

Assess values alignment: Evaluate whether the candidate's values align with the organization's core values. This can be done through questions or assessments that focus on key values such as integrity, accountability, and innovation.

Evaluate communication style: Observe how the candidate communicates during the interview process. Are they able to effectively communicate and collaborate with team members? Do they demonstrate active listening skills?

Consider organizational fit: Consider if the candidate's previous work experience and industry knowledge align with the organization's goals and values. Look for candidates who have a passion for the industry and a strong understanding of the company's mission.

Conduct cultural fit assessments: This can include personality tests or assessments that measure cultural fit. These assessments can provide additional insights into a candidate's compatibility with the organization's culture.

Seek feedback from the team: Involve the hiring manager and other team members in the decision-making process. Gather feedback on the candidate's interactions during the interview process to gain different perspectives on their cultural fit.

Use real-world examples: Provide real-world scenarios and ask the candidate how they would handle them. This can help assess their problem-solving abilities and how they would navigate cultural challenges within the organization.

Summarize the candidate's fit: After considering all the above factors, summarize the candidate's cultural fit based on their values, communication style, industry knowledge, and feedback from the team. Determine if they align with the organization's culture and if they would contribute positively to the team dynamic.

What role do skills assessments play in your candidate evaluation process?

Answer

Skills assessments play a crucial role in our candidate evaluation process as a Talent Acquisition Specialist specializing in top-tier IT companies. Here are the key roles skills assessments play in our process:

• Objective evaluation: Skills assessments help us objectively evaluate a candidate's technical skills and knowledge, ensuring that they have the expertise required for the role.

• Differentiation: In a highly competitive field like IT, skills assessments help us differentiate between candidates with similar qualifications. They provide a standardized measure of a candidate's abilities, allowing us to compare and rank them effectively.

• Validation of claims: Candidates often mention their skills and experience in their resumes or interviews. Skills assessments provide a way to validate these claims and ensure that candidates possess the skills they claim to have.

• Identifying skill gaps: Skills assessments help us identify any skill gaps or areas where a candidate may require further training or development. This information is valuable in making informed decisions about candidate suitability and potential for growth.

• Efficient screening process: By using skills assessments early in the evaluation process, we can efficiently screen a large pool of candidates and focus our attention on those who demonstrate the required skills and knowledge.

• Reducing bias: Skills assessments provide an objective measure of a candidate's abilities, reducing the potential for bias in the evaluation process. This helps ensure a fair and equitable assessment of all candidates.

Interviewing and Selection

Interviewing and selection are critical steps in the talent acquisition process as they help identify the best candidates for a particular role. The interviewing and selection process typically involves the following steps:

• Reviewing resumes and applications: This step involves screening resumes and applications to shortlist candidates who meet the job requirements. This can be done by assessing their skills, experience, and qualifications.

• Conducting phone screens: Phone screens are often conducted to further assess candidates' qualifications, communication skills, and fit for the role. This step helps filter out candidates who may not be a good fit for the position.

• In-person interviews: In-person interviews are typically conducted to evaluate candidates' technical skills, problem-solving abilities, and cultural fit. This step may involve multiple rounds of interviews with different stakeholders, such as hiring managers, team members, and executives.

• Assessments and tests: To ensure candidates have the necessary skills and knowledge for the role, assessments and tests may be administered. These can include technical tests, aptitude tests, and personality assessments.

• Reference checks: Reference checks are conducted to verify the information provided by candidates and gather insights from their previous employers or colleagues. This step helps validate candidates' qualifications and work history.

Real-world example:
As a Talent Acquisition Specialist specializing in top-tier IT companies, I have been involved in the interviewing and selection process for various technical roles. For example, when hiring software engineers, we typically review their resumes and assess their technical skills through phone screens and in-person coding interviews. We also administer coding assessments to evaluate their problem-solving abilities and conduct reference checks to gather feedback from their previous supervisors. This thorough selection process ensures that we hire the most qualified candidates who can excel in their roles.

How do you structure and conduct effective interviews?

Answer

To structure and conduct effective interviews as a Talent Acquisition Specialist specializing in top-tier IT companies, you can follow these steps:

• Define the job requirements and create a job description: Start by understanding the specific skills, experience, and qualifications required for the position. This will help you create a job description that accurately reflects the role and attracts the right candidates.

• Prepare interview questions: Develop a list of interview questions that assess the candidate's technical skills, problem-solving abilities, teamwork, and cultural fit. Use a mix of behavioral and situational questions to evaluate their past experiences and how they would handle different scenarios.

• Conduct phone screenings: Before bringing candidates in for an in-person interview, conduct phone screenings to assess their basic qualifications and interest in the role. This will help you shortlist candidates and save time during the later stages of the hiring process.

• Plan the interview format: Decide on the interview format based on the position and your company's preferences. It can be a one-on-one interview, panel interview, or a combination of different interview types. Consider including technical assessments or coding exercises to evaluate the candidate's skills.

• Create a structured interview guide: Prepare a structured interview guide that includes all the questions you plan to ask. This will ensure consistency across interviews and help you compare candidates objectively.

• Conduct the interview: During the interview, create a welcoming and comfortable environment for the candidate. Start with introductions and an overview of the interview process. Ask the prepared questions and actively listen to the candidate's responses. Take notes to refer back to later.

• Assess candidate fit: Evaluate the candidate's skills, experience, and cultural fit based on their responses. Use a scoring system or evaluation criteria to objectively compare candidates. Look for evidence of their ability to solve problems, work in a team, and adapt to different situations.

• Provide information about the role and company: Give candidates an opportunity to ask questions and provide them with information about the role, team, and company culture. This will help them make an informed decision if they receive an offer.

• Follow up with candidates: After the interview, follow up with candidates to provide feedback and updates on the hiring process. This helps maintain a positive candidate experience and keeps them engaged with your company.

Real-world example:
For example, let's say you are hiring a Software Engineer for a top-tier IT company. You would start by defining the technical skills, programming languages, and experience required for the role. Based on this, you would create a job description that accurately reflects the position. Next, you would prepare interview questions that assess the candidate's coding abilities, problem-solving skills, and experience with relevant technologies. During the interview, you would ask the prepared questions and evaluate the candidate's responses. Additionally, you might include a coding exercise to assess their programming skills. You would also provide information about the company's projects, team structure, and growth opportunities to help the candidate make an informed decision. Finally, you would follow up with the candidate to provide feedback and updates on the hiring process.

Summary: To structure and conduct effective interviews as a Talent Acquisition Specialist specializing in top-tier IT companies, define job requirements, prepare interview questions, conduct phone screenings, plan the interview format, create a structured interview guide, conduct the interview, assess candidate fit, provide information about the role and company, follow up with candidates.

An example of when you successfully identified a high-potential candidate during an interview?

Answer

During an interview for a Talent Acquisition Specialist role at a top-tier IT company, I encountered a candidate who stood out as a high-potential individual. Here is an example of how I successfully identified this candidate:

I was conducting a panel interview for a software engineering position, and one candidate's responses and behavior caught my attention. Here are the key indicators that led me to identify them as a high-potential candidate:

• Clear and concise communication: The candidate effectively communicated their ideas and experiences, demonstrating excellent verbal and written communication skills. They were able to explain complex technical concepts in a way that was easy to understand.

• Depth of technical knowledge: The candidate displayed a deep understanding of various programming languages, frameworks, and software development methodologies. They were able to provide detailed explanations and examples for each technical question asked.

• Problem-solving abilities: When presented with a hypothetical scenario, the candidate showcased their ability to analyze the situation, break it down into smaller components, and propose practical solutions. They demonstrated a logical and structured approach to problem-solving.

• Enthusiasm and passion: The candidate displayed a genuine passion for software engineering and the IT industry as a whole. They expressed excitement about staying up-to-date with the latest technologies and constantly learning and improving their skills.

• Cultural fit: The candidate's values and work ethic aligned with the company's culture. They emphasized the importance of collaboration, teamwork, and continuous improvement, which are core values of the organization.

Based on these observations, I recommended moving this candidate forward in the hiring process. They ultimately proved to be a high-performing employee who made significant contributions to the company's projects and team dynamics.

What techniques do you use to evaluate a candidate's soft skills?

Answer

Conducting behavioral interviews to assess how candidates have handled specific situations in the past. For example, asking questions like 'Tell me about a time when you had to deal with a difficult coworker' can provide insights into a candidate's communication and conflict resolution skills.

Using role-playing exercises to simulate real-life scenarios. This can help evaluate a candidate's ability to handle interpersonal relationships, problem-solving, and decision-making. For instance, asking candidates to act out a customer service interaction can reveal their empathy, patience, and problem-solving skills.

Administering psychometric assessments to measure personality traits and behavioral tendencies. These assessments can provide objective data on a candidate's communication style, teamwork orientation, leadership potential, and other soft skills.

Requesting references from previous employers or colleagues to gain insights into a candidate's soft skills. Speaking to people who have worked closely with the candidate can provide valuable information about their teamwork, communication, and adaptability.

Observing a candidate's non-verbal cues and body language during the interview. This can give indications of their active listening skills, confidence, and ability to connect with others.

Asking open-ended questions that require candidates to provide detailed responses. This can help assess their communication skills, critical thinking ability, and problem-solving approach. For example, asking candidates to describe a challenging project they worked on and how they overcame obstacles can reveal their ability to effectively communicate complex ideas and navigate difficult situations.

How do you ensure a positive candidate experience during the interview process?

Answer

Communicate clearly and promptly: Provide clear instructions and information about the interview process, including the date, time, location, and any necessary preparation. Respond promptly to candidate inquiries or concerns.

Create a welcoming atmosphere: Make candidates feel comfortable and welcome from the moment they arrive. Greet them warmly, offer them a beverage, and introduce them to the interview panel or team members.

Provide a structured and organized interview: Ensure that the interview is well-planned and organized. Have a clear agenda, provide all necessary materials, and give candidates an overview of what to expect.

Ask relevant and meaningful questions: Prepare a set of questions that are relevant to the role and provide insight into the candidate's skills, experience, and fit for the company culture. Avoid asking irrelevant or discriminatory questions.

Listen actively and engage in conversation: Show genuine interest in the candidate's responses and actively engage in conversation. Ask follow-up questions and encourage candidates to expand on their answers.

Offer transparency and feedback: Be transparent about the interview process, including the timeline for decision-making. After the interview, provide timely and constructive feedback to candidates, regardless of the outcome.

Summarize the answer: To ensure a positive candidate experience during the interview process, it is important to communicate clearly and promptly, create a welcoming atmosphere, provide a structured and organized interview, ask relevant and meaningful questions, listen actively and engage in conversation, offer transparency and feedback.

Employer Branding

Employer branding refers to the process of promoting a company as an attractive employer to both current and potential employees. It involves creating a positive and appealing image of the company's culture, values, and work environment.

A strong employer brand can help attract and retain top talent, enhance the company's reputation, and differentiate it from competitors.

Employer branding strategies often include the following elements:

1. Company Culture: Highlighting the company's unique culture and values, such as flexible work arrangements, employee development programs, and inclusive policies.

2. Employee Value Proposition (EVP): Defining and communicating the benefits and rewards employees can expect, such as competitive salaries, career growth opportunities, and work-life balance.

3. Employee Testimonials: Showcasing real-life stories and testimonials from current employees to demonstrate their positive experiences and satisfaction with the company.

4. Online Presence: Building and maintaining a strong online presence through social media platforms, company websites, and job boards to reach and engage with potential candidates.

5. Recruitment Marketing: Utilizing marketing techniques to promote the company's brand, such as creating compelling job descriptions, targeted advertising campaigns, and engaging content.

6. Candidate Experience: Ensuring a positive and seamless experience for candidates throughout the recruitment process, including clear communication, timely feedback, and a personalized approach.

Real-world examples of employer branding in top-tier IT companies include:

• Google: Known for its innovative and inclusive culture, Google emphasizes its employee perks, such as free meals, on-site gyms, and flexible work arrangements. They also highlight their commitment to employee development and work-life balance.

• Microsoft: Microsoft focuses on its mission to empower every person and organization on the planet to achieve more. They

highlight their employee benefits, such as competitive salaries, comprehensive health plans, and opportunities for career growth.
• Amazon: Amazon promotes its fast-paced and customer-centric culture, offering competitive compensation packages, extensive training programs, and opportunities to work on cutting-edge technologies.
Summarized answer:
Employer branding is the process of promoting a company as an attractive employer. It involves showcasing the company's culture, values, and benefits to attract and retain top talent. Strategies include highlighting company culture, defining employee value propositions, using employee testimonials, maintaining an online presence, utilizing recruitment marketing techniques, and ensuring a positive candidate experience.

How do you contribute to building and promoting the employer brand?

Answer

As a Talent Acquisition Specialist specializing in top-tier IT companies, I play a crucial role in building and promoting the employer brand. Here are some ways in which I contribute to this process:
1. Developing a strong employer value proposition (EVP): I work closely with the company's leadership team and HR department to understand the unique selling points of the organization and its culture. Based on this, I develop a compelling EVP that highlights the benefits and opportunities of working for the company.
2. Crafting engaging job descriptions: I ensure that job descriptions are not just a list of requirements, but also highlight the company's culture, values, and mission. This helps attract candidates who align with the organization's goals and values.
3. Creating a positive candidate experience: I strive to provide a positive and seamless experience to candidates throughout the recruitment process. This includes clear communication, timely feedback, and personalized interactions. A positive experience leaves a lasting impression on candidates and enhances the employer brand.

4. Leveraging social media and online platforms: I utilize social media platforms, such as LinkedIn, Twitter, and Facebook, to showcase the company's culture, employee testimonials, and career opportunities. This helps create a strong online presence and reach a wider audience of potential candidates.

5. Building relationships with top talent: I actively network and engage with top talent in the industry, attending industry events, and participating in online communities. Building relationships with sought-after professionals not only enhances the employer brand but also helps attract top talent to the organization.

6. Monitoring and managing employer brand reputation: I regularly monitor online platforms and review sites to understand how the company is perceived by current and former employees. This allows me to address any negative feedback or concerns and take proactive steps to improve the employer brand.

By implementing these strategies, I contribute to building and promoting a strong employer brand, attracting top talent to the organization.

Discuss your experience with social media in employer branding?

Answer

I have extensive experience in using social media platforms for employer branding purposes as a Talent Acquisition Specialist specializing in top-tier IT companies.

Some of the key strategies and tactics I have employed include:

1. Creating compelling and engaging employer brand content: I have developed and curated content that showcases the company's culture, values, and employee experiences. This includes videos, blog posts, and infographics that highlight the unique aspects of working at the company.

2. Leveraging social media platforms: I have utilized platforms like LinkedIn, Facebook, Twitter, and Instagram to reach a wide audience of potential candidates. By sharing the employer brand content and engaging with followers, I have been able to increase brand awareness and attract top talent.

3. Targeted advertising campaigns: I have run targeted advertising campaigns on social media platforms to reach specific demographics and job functions. By tailoring the messaging and visuals to resonate with the target audience, I have been able to attract candidates with the right skills and experience.

4. Employee advocacy programs: I have encouraged employees to share their experiences and promote the employer brand on social media. This not only helps in building credibility but also expands the reach of the employer brand to their networks.

5. Monitoring and analyzing performance: I regularly monitor the performance of social media campaigns and analyze metrics such as reach, engagement, and conversion rates. This helps me understand what strategies are working well and make data-driven decisions for future campaigns.

One real-world example of my experience with social media in employer branding is when I worked for a top IT company. We created a series of videos featuring employees talking about their career growth and development opportunities within the company. These videos were shared on LinkedIn and Facebook, and we saw a significant increase in engagement and applications from top-tier IT professionals.

Summarizing my experience, I have successfully utilized social media platforms for employer branding purposes by creating compelling content, leveraging various platforms, running targeted campaigns, promoting employee advocacy, and analyzing performance metrics.

How do you leverage employee testimonials in recruitment efforts?

Answer

Employee testimonials can be a powerful tool in recruitment efforts as they provide an authentic and genuine perspective of the company culture and work environment. Here are some ways to leverage employee testimonials:

1. Incorporate testimonials in job postings: Include quotes or snippets from employee testimonials in job postings to give potential

candidates a glimpse of what it's like to work at the company. This can help attract candidates who resonate with the values and experiences shared by current employees.

2. Create a dedicated testimonials page on the company website: Build a testimonials page on the company website where potential candidates can read and watch videos of current employees sharing their experiences. This can provide valuable insights into the company culture and help candidates make an informed decision.

3. Share testimonials on social media platforms: Utilize social media platforms like LinkedIn, Twitter, and Instagram to share employee testimonials. This can help reach a wider audience and create a positive brand image among potential candidates.

4. Include testimonials in recruitment marketing campaigns: Use employee testimonials in recruitment marketing campaigns, such as email newsletters, blog posts, or online advertisements. This can help build credibility and trust among potential candidates.

5. Encourage employees to share testimonials on their personal networks: Encourage employees to share their testimonials on their personal social media networks or professional platforms like LinkedIn. This can help reach passive candidates who may not actively be looking for a job but could be interested in joining the company based on the positive experiences shared by current employees.

6. Use video testimonials: Video testimonials can be particularly impactful as they allow candidates to see and hear current employees firsthand. Consider creating a series of video testimonials highlighting different aspects of the company culture and work environment.

By leveraging employee testimonials in recruitment efforts, companies can provide an authentic and relatable perspective to potential candidates, helping them make informed decisions and attracting top talent.

What strategies do you use to attract top talent to the organization?

Answer

Develop a strong employer brand: Creating a positive and attractive employer brand helps in attracting top talent. This can be achieved by showcasing the company's culture, values, and employee testimonials. Using social media platforms like LinkedIn, Glassdoor, and Indeed to share employee experiences and success stories can also help in building a strong employer brand.

Utilize targeted job postings: Posting job openings on niche job boards and industry-specific websites can help in reaching out to top talent. It is important to tailor the job descriptions to highlight the unique aspects and opportunities offered by the organization.

Leverage employee referrals: Encouraging employees to refer potential candidates can be an effective way to attract top talent. Offering referral bonuses or incentives can incentivize employees to actively participate in the referral program.

Engage with passive candidates: Actively reaching out to passive candidates who may not be actively looking for a job but possess the desired skill set can help in attracting top talent. This can be done through networking events, industry conferences, and online communities.

Build relationships with universities: Partnering with universities and colleges can provide access to fresh talent and help in attracting top graduates. Participating in career fairs, offering internships, and conducting campus recruitment drives can help in building relationships with universities.

Offer competitive compensation and benefits: Providing competitive salary packages, performance-based incentives, and attractive benefits can make the organization more appealing to top talent. Conducting regular market research to ensure that the compensation packages are in line with industry standards is crucial.

Provide growth and development opportunities: Highlighting the opportunities for career growth, skill development, and learning within the organization can attract top talent. Offering mentorship programs, training sessions, and clear career progression paths can showcase the organization's commitment to employee development.

Summary: To attract top talent to the organization, it is important to develop a strong employer brand, utilize targeted job postings, leverage employee referrals, engage with passive candidates, build relationships with universities, offer competitive compensation and benefits, and provide growth and development opportunities.

Talent Pipelines and Networking

Answer

Talent pipelines and networking are crucial aspects of talent acquisition in top-tier IT companies.

A talent pipeline refers to a pool of potential candidates who have been identified and nurtured for future job opportunities within an organization.

Networking, on the other hand, involves building and maintaining professional relationships with individuals who may be potential candidates or sources of referrals.

The combination of talent pipelines and networking allows talent acquisition specialists to proactively identify and engage with high-quality candidates.

Here are some key points to consider when it comes to talent pipelines and networking in the context of top-tier IT companies:

1. Developing Talent Pipelines:

• Talent acquisition specialists need to proactively identify and engage with potential candidates who possess the skills and qualifications required by top-tier IT companies.

• This can be done through various methods, such as attending industry events, participating in online communities, and leveraging social media platforms like LinkedIn.

• By building relationships with potential candidates, talent acquisition specialists can keep them informed about future job opportunities and maintain a pipeline of talent for the organization.

2. Leveraging Networking:

• Networking plays a crucial role in talent acquisition, as it allows talent acquisition specialists to tap into their professional connections to identify potential candidates.

• Building a strong network involves attending industry events, joining professional associations, and actively engaging on social media platforms.

• Through networking, talent acquisition specialists can gain insights into the job market, industry trends, and potential candidates who may not be actively looking for new opportunities.

3. Engaging Passive Candidates:

- Talent acquisition specialists in top-tier IT companies often target passive candidates who are employed but may be open to new opportunities.
- By leveraging their talent pipelines and networking connections, talent acquisition specialists can identify and approach passive candidates with relevant job opportunities.
- Engaging passive candidates requires a personalized approach and showcasing the unique value proposition of the organization to attract their interest.

In summary, talent pipelines and networking are essential strategies for talent acquisition specialists in top-tier IT companies. By proactively identifying and engaging with potential candidates, leveraging professional networks, and targeting passive candidates, talent acquisition specialists can build a strong pool of high-quality talent for their organizations.

How do you build and maintain a talent pipeline for future hiring needs?

Answer

To build and maintain a talent pipeline for future hiring needs as a Talent Acquisition Specialist specializing in top-tier IT companies, you can follow these steps:

- Identify the key skills and qualifications required for the future roles in your organization. This could include technical skills, industry-specific knowledge, and soft skills.
- Develop a strong employer brand that attracts top talent. This can be done through showcasing your company culture, values, and success stories.
- Actively source and engage with potential candidates through various channels such as job boards, social media platforms, networking events, and referrals.
- Build relationships with universities, coding bootcamps, and other educational institutions to tap into the emerging talent pool.
- Implement a robust candidate relationship management system to stay in touch with passive candidates and nurture relationships over time.

• Create a talent pipeline database to track and manage potential candidates for future roles.
• Regularly update and maintain the talent pipeline database with new candidate information and feedback from interviews and assessments.
• Provide ongoing training and development opportunities for existing employees to retain top talent and build a strong internal talent pipeline.
• Continuously evaluate and optimize your talent acquisition strategies based on metrics such as time-to-fill, quality of hires, and candidate satisfaction.
• Collaborate with hiring managers and other stakeholders to understand their future hiring needs and align your talent pipeline accordingly.

Discuss your experience with networking events and industry conferences?

Answer

I have extensive experience attending networking events and industry conferences as a Talent Acquisition Specialist specializing in top-tier IT companies. Here are some key points about my experience:
• I have attended various networking events and industry conferences in the IT industry, such as TechExpo and the IT Leadership Summit.
• At these events, I have had the opportunity to connect with top IT professionals, including software engineers, data scientists, and IT managers.
• I have successfully built relationships with industry leaders and gained valuable insights into the latest trends and technologies in the IT field.
• Through networking events and industry conferences, I have been able to identify potential candidates for open positions and engage in meaningful conversations about their skills and experiences.
• I have also utilized these events to promote my company's employer brand and attract top talent to our organization.

• Additionally, I have participated as a speaker or panelist at some industry conferences, sharing my expertise in talent acquisition and providing valuable insights to the audience.
• I always make sure to follow up with the contacts I meet at these events, whether it's through LinkedIn or email, to maintain relationships and explore potential collaboration opportunities.

How do you engage with candidates who are not an immediate fit but may be in the future?

Answer

Maintain regular communication with the candidate to keep them engaged and interested in future opportunities.

Provide them with updates on the company, industry trends, and any relevant news that may be of interest to them.

Offer them the opportunity to attend company events or webinars to stay connected and learn more about the organization.

Invite them to join the company's talent community or newsletter to receive updates on job openings and company updates.

Offer to provide feedback and guidance on areas for improvement or additional skills they may need to be considered for future roles.

Consider them for other roles within the organization that may be a better fit or relevant to their skills and experience.

Maintain a positive and professional relationship with the candidate, even if they are not an immediate fit, as they may refer other candidates or become a potential fit in the future.

What methods do you use to keep in touch with passive candidates?

Answer

As a Talent Acquisition Specialist specializing in top-tier IT companies, I use a variety of methods to keep in touch with passive candidates:
• Regular email communication: Sending personalized emails to passive candidates to keep them updated on relevant job openings,

company updates, and industry news. This helps to maintain a connection and keep them engaged with the company.

• Social media engagement: Actively connecting with passive candidates on professional social media platforms such as LinkedIn and Twitter. Liking, commenting, and sharing their posts can help to establish a relationship and keep them interested in potential opportunities with the company.

• Networking events: Attending industry-specific networking events and conferences to meet passive candidates in person and build relationships. This allows for more personal and direct communication, making it easier to stay connected.

• Newsletter subscriptions: Encouraging passive candidates to subscribe to the company's newsletter or blog. This way, they receive regular updates on the company's activities and can stay informed about potential job opportunities.

• Talent community platforms: Utilizing talent community platforms where passive candidates can join and stay connected with the company. These platforms often provide forums, webinars, and other resources to engage candidates and keep them interested.

• Personalized follow-ups: Sending personalized follow-up messages or making phone calls to passive candidates after initial interactions or interviews. This shows continued interest and keeps the lines of communication open.

By using these methods, I ensure that passive candidates feel valued and engaged with the company, increasing the chances of them considering future opportunities.

Collaboration with Hiring Managers

Collaboration with hiring managers is essential for a talent acquisition specialist specializing in top-tier IT companies. By working closely with hiring managers, the talent acquisition specialist can ensure a smooth and efficient recruitment process. Here are some key points to consider when collaborating with hiring managers:

• Establishing clear communication channels: It is important to establish regular communication channels with hiring managers to ensure that both parties are on the same page. This can include regular meetings, email updates, or project management tools.

• Understanding the hiring needs: The talent acquisition specialist should have a deep understanding of the hiring needs of the hiring managers. This includes understanding the specific skills and qualifications required for each position, as well as any specific preferences or requirements.

• Providing regular updates and feedback: The talent acquisition specialist should provide regular updates to hiring managers on the progress of the recruitment process. This can include updates on the number of candidates identified, the status of interviews, and any challenges or roadblocks that may arise.

• Collaborating on job descriptions and candidate profiles: The talent acquisition specialist should work closely with hiring managers to develop job descriptions and candidate profiles that accurately reflect the requirements of the position. This collaboration ensures that the job advertisement attracts the right candidates and that the candidate evaluation process is aligned with the hiring manager's expectations.

• Identifying and addressing recruitment challenges: Collaboration with hiring managers also involves identifying and addressing any challenges that may arise during the recruitment process. This can include issues such as a shortage of qualified candidates, a slow hiring process, or difficulties in attracting top talent. By working together, the talent acquisition specialist and hiring manager can develop strategies to overcome these challenges and ensure a successful recruitment process.

• Building a strong working relationship: Collaboration with hiring managers is not just about the recruitment process, but also about building a strong working relationship. This involves understanding the hiring manager's preferences and communication style, as well as developing trust and rapport. A strong working relationship can lead to better collaboration and a more successful recruitment process.

How do you establish strong partnerships with hiring managers?

Answer

Establishing strong partnerships with hiring managers is crucial for a Talent Acquisition Specialist specializing in top-tier IT companies. Here are some effective strategies to do so:

• Understand their needs: Take the time to thoroughly understand the hiring manager's requirements, including the technical skills, experience, and cultural fit they are seeking in candidates. This will enable you to source and present the most suitable candidates.

• Regular communication: Maintain open and transparent communication with hiring managers throughout the recruitment process. This includes providing regular updates on the status of candidates, sharing feedback, and addressing any concerns or questions they may have. Regular check-ins can help build trust and collaboration.

• Collaborative approach: Work closely with hiring managers as partners in the recruitment process. Involve them in candidate screening, interviews, and decision-making. Seek their input and expertise to ensure a collaborative and inclusive hiring process.

• Provide data-driven insights: Use data and analytics to provide hiring managers with insights on market trends, candidate availability, and competitive landscape. This information can help them make informed decisions and adjust their hiring strategies accordingly.

• Continuous feedback loop: Establish a feedback loop with hiring managers to gather their feedback on the quality of candidates, interview process, and overall recruitment experience. Actively listen to their suggestions and implement improvements to enhance the partnership.

By following these strategies, a Talent Acquisition Specialist can establish strong partnerships with hiring managers and contribute to the success of their organization's talent acquisition efforts.

Share an example of a challenging hiring manager relationship you successfully navigated?

Answer

In my previous role as a Talent Acquisition Specialist specializing in top-tier IT companies, I encountered a challenging hiring manager relationship with a senior executive at a leading tech firm.

The hiring manager had a reputation for being extremely demanding and had high expectations for the candidates I presented.

To successfully navigate this relationship, I implemented several strategies:

• I took the time to thoroughly understand the hiring manager's expectations, preferences, and requirements for the role.

• I proactively communicated with the hiring manager throughout the recruitment process, providing regular updates on candidate progress and addressing any concerns or questions.

• I collaborated closely with the hiring manager to identify the key competencies and skills required for the role, ensuring alignment between their expectations and the candidates I sourced.

• I leveraged my network and utilized targeted sourcing strategies to identify top-tier candidates who met the hiring manager's criteria.

• I presented a shortlist of qualified candidates that closely matched the hiring manager's requirements, providing detailed insights and recommendations for each candidate.

• I facilitated efficient and effective interview processes, coordinating schedules and providing guidance to both the hiring manager and the candidates.

• I maintained a proactive and professional approach, demonstrating my commitment to finding the best-fit candidates for the role.

By implementing these strategies, I was able to successfully navigate the challenging hiring manager relationship and secure high-quality candidates for the tech firm.

How do you manage conflicting priorities and expectations from hiring managers?

Answer

Prioritize tasks based on urgency and importance
Communicate with hiring managers to understand their expectations and priorities
Negotiate and find common ground when conflicting priorities arise
Provide regular updates and progress reports to hiring managers
Seek feedback and clarify expectations to ensure alignment
Manage time effectively and set realistic expectations
Delegate tasks when necessary
Use project management tools and techniques to organize and track tasks

How do you ensure alignment between hiring goals and overall business objectives?

Answer

To ensure alignment between hiring goals and overall business objectives as a Talent Acquisition Specialist specializing in top-tier IT companies, I would follow the following steps:
1. Understand the business objectives: Firstly, I would thoroughly understand the overall business objectives of the company. This involves reviewing the company's mission, vision, and strategic goals. By having a clear understanding of what the company wants to achieve, I can align the hiring goals to support those objectives.
2. Collaborate with key stakeholders: I would actively engage with key stakeholders such as department heads, hiring managers, and executives. By having open and transparent communication, I can gain insights into their specific hiring needs and how it aligns with the broader business objectives.
3. Conduct a gap analysis: Next, I would conduct a gap analysis to identify any gaps between the current workforce and the desired workforce needed to achieve the business objectives. This involves assessing the skills, experience, and competencies required for each role and comparing it to the existing talent pool.

4. Develop a hiring strategy: Based on the gap analysis, I would develop a comprehensive hiring strategy that outlines the steps and resources needed to attract, assess, and select the right candidates. This strategy would be aligned with the overall business objectives, ensuring that the hiring goals are directly contributing to the success of the company.

5. Implement measurement and evaluation: To ensure ongoing alignment, I would establish clear metrics and KPIs to measure the effectiveness of the hiring process. This could include metrics such as time-to-fill, quality of hire, and retention rates. Regular evaluation and analysis of these metrics would allow me to make data-driven decisions and make adjustments as needed to stay aligned with the business objectives.

6. Continuous feedback and improvement: Lastly, I would seek feedback from hiring managers and candidates to continuously improve the hiring process. By understanding their experiences and perspectives, I can identify areas for improvement and make necessary adjustments to better align hiring goals with the overall business objectives.

Data-Driven Recruiting

Data-driven recruiting is a recruitment strategy that uses data and analytics to drive decision-making in the talent acquisition process. It involves collecting and analyzing data on candidates, job postings, sourcing channels, and other relevant metrics to optimize the recruitment process and improve hiring outcomes.

Here are some key components of data-driven recruiting:

• Metrics and KPIs: Data-driven recruiting relies on the use of metrics and key performance indicators (KPIs) to measure and track the effectiveness of recruiting efforts. These can include metrics such as time-to-fill, cost-per-hire, quality of hire, and source of hire.

• Candidate sourcing: Data-driven recruiting involves analyzing data on sourcing channels to identify the most effective channels for attracting top talent. This could include analyzing data on job boards, social media platforms, employee referrals, and external agencies to determine which sources yield the highest quality candidates.

• Candidate assessment: Data-driven recruiting uses data and analytics to assess candidate fit and potential. This could involve using pre-employment assessments, analyzing candidate resumes and profiles, and conducting structured interviews with standardized evaluation criteria.

• Predictive analytics: Data-driven recruiting leverages predictive analytics to forecast future hiring needs and identify potential bottlenecks or challenges in the hiring process. By analyzing historical data and trends, recruiters can make data-driven decisions on workforce planning, talent pipelining, and candidate engagement strategies.

Real-world example: A talent acquisition specialist specializing in top-tier IT companies could use data-driven recruiting to optimize their hiring process. They could analyze data on candidate sourcing channels to determine which channels yield the highest quality candidates for IT roles. They could also use data to assess candidate fit and potential, identifying the key skills and traits that are most predictive of success in their organization. By using data and analytics, they can make informed decisions on where to invest their recruitment resources and how to improve their hiring outcomes.

What key performance indicators (KPIs) do you track in recruitment?

Answer

Time-to-fill: This KPI measures the average time it takes to fill a vacant position. It is important to track this metric to ensure that the recruitment process is efficient and does not unnecessarily delay the hiring process. For example, a Talent Acquisition Specialist specializing in top-tier IT companies may aim to have a time-to-fill of 30 days for a software engineer position.

Cost-per-hire: This KPI measures the average cost incurred to fill a vacant position. It includes expenses such as advertising costs, recruitment agency fees, and employee referral rewards. By tracking this metric, the Talent Acquisition Specialist can evaluate the effectiveness of different recruitment channels and make data-driven decisions to optimize recruitment costs.

Quality of hire: This KPI measures the performance and fit of new hires in the organization. It can be evaluated through factors such as employee performance ratings, retention rates, and feedback from managers. The Talent Acquisition Specialist can track this metric to assess the effectiveness of the recruitment process in attracting and selecting high-quality candidates.

Source of hire: This KPI tracks the effectiveness of different recruitment sources in generating successful hires. It helps the Talent Acquisition Specialist understand which channels, such as job boards, social media, or employee referrals, are most effective in attracting qualified candidates. By analyzing this data, the specialist can allocate resources and focus on the most successful sources of hire.

Offer acceptance rate: This KPI measures the percentage of job offers that are accepted by candidates. A low offer acceptance rate may indicate issues with the attractiveness of the job offer or the recruitment process. The Talent Acquisition Specialist can track this metric to identify areas for improvement and make adjustments to increase the acceptance rate.

Diversity hiring: This KPI measures the representation of diverse candidates in the recruitment process. It tracks the percentage of candidates from underrepresented groups who are sourced, interviewed, and hired. By tracking this metric, the Talent Acquisition Specialist can ensure diversity and inclusion goals are met and identify any potential biases or gaps in the recruitment process.

Discuss a situation where you used data to optimize the recruitment process?

Answer

In my role as a Talent Acquisition Specialist specializing in top-tier IT companies, I have frequently utilized data to optimize the recruitment process. One particular situation that stands out is when we were looking to hire software engineers for a leading tech company.

To optimize the recruitment process, I employed data in the following ways:

• Conducted a thorough analysis of past hiring data: I reviewed previous hiring data to identify patterns and trends. This helped me understand the success rate of different recruitment channels, such as job boards, employee referrals, and social media platforms.

• Utilized applicant tracking system (ATS) data: We used an ATS to track applicant data and measure the effectiveness of various recruitment strategies. By analyzing the data from the ATS, we were able to identify bottlenecks in the recruitment process and make necessary adjustments.

• Implemented data-driven sourcing strategies: By analyzing data on the most successful hires, we identified the key skills and attributes that were common among them. Based on this analysis, we optimized our job descriptions and targeted specific talent pools to attract candidates with the desired qualifications.

• Monitored recruitment metrics: We tracked and analyzed various recruitment metrics, such as time-to-fill, cost-per-hire, and quality-of-hire. By monitoring these metrics, we could identify areas of improvement and make data-driven decisions to optimize the recruitment process.

As a result of using data to optimize the recruitment process, we experienced several benefits:

• Increased efficiency: By identifying the most effective recruitment channels and strategies, we were able to streamline the hiring process and reduce time-to-fill.
• Improved quality of hires: By analyzing the data on successful hires, we were able to target candidates with the right skills and qualifications, leading to a higher quality of hires.
• Cost savings: By optimizing recruitment strategies and reducing time-to-fill, we were able to minimize recruitment costs.

In summary, by utilizing data in the recruitment process, we were able to make informed decisions, improve efficiency, and attract high-quality candidates. Data analysis played a crucial role in optimizing the recruitment process for top-tier IT companies.

How do you analyze recruitment metrics to improve hiring outcomes?

Answer
Identify the key recruitment metrics: Begin by identifying the key metrics that are relevant to your talent acquisition process. These metrics can include time to hire, cost per hire, applicant to hire ratio, quality of hire, and retention rate.

Gather data: Collect data on these metrics from various sources such as applicant tracking systems, HR databases, and performance management systems. Ensure that the data is accurate and up-to-date.

Analyze the data: Once you have gathered the data, analyze it to identify patterns, trends, and areas of improvement. Look for insights that can help you make informed decisions about your recruitment process.

Use benchmarking: Compare your recruitment metrics with industry benchmarks to understand how you are performing against your competitors. This can help you identify areas where you are lagging behind and take corrective actions.

Identify areas for improvement: Based on your analysis and benchmarking, identify specific areas for improvement in your recruitment process. This could be reducing time to hire, lowering cost per hire, or improving the quality of candidates.

Implement changes: Once you have identified areas for improvement, develop and implement strategies to address them. This could involve streamlining your recruitment process, leveraging technology, or improving your employer brand.

Monitor and measure: Continuously monitor and measure the impact of the changes you have implemented. Track the recruitment metrics over time to see if there is any improvement in hiring outcomes.

Make data-driven decisions: Use the insights from your analysis and monitoring to make data-driven decisions about your recruitment process. Adjust your strategies as needed to optimize your hiring outcomes.

What role does data play in your decision-making process?

Answer

Data plays a crucial role in my decision-making process as a Talent Acquisition Specialist specializing in top-tier IT companies. Here is how data influences my decisions:

Data helps me identify the skills and qualifications that are most in demand in the IT industry. By analyzing job market data and industry trends, I can determine the specific skills that top-tier IT companies are looking for in candidates.

Data also helps me evaluate the success of my recruitment strategies. I track metrics such as time-to-fill, cost-per-hire, and quality-of-hire to assess the effectiveness of different sourcing channels and recruitment methods. This allows me to make data-driven decisions about which strategies to prioritize and invest more resources in.

Data analysis plays a crucial role in the screening and selection process. By leveraging applicant tracking systems and data analytics tools, I can quickly filter and analyze large volumes of resumes to identify the most qualified candidates. This saves time and ensures that I am considering candidates who meet the specific requirements of the job.

Data also helps me assess the performance and potential of candidates during the interview process. For example, I may use pre-employment assessments and behavioral interview questions to gather data on a candidate's technical skills, problem-solving abilities, and cultural fit. This data provides valuable insights that inform my decision-making when selecting candidates for further consideration.

Data analysis is also important in evaluating the effectiveness of my overall talent acquisition strategy. By tracking key performance indicators and analyzing recruitment data, I can identify areas for improvement and make data-driven decisions to optimize my processes.

Real-world example: Let's say I am recruiting for a top-tier IT company that is focused on developing artificial intelligence solutions. By analyzing data on AI job postings and industry reports, I can identify the specific AI skills and qualifications that are in high demand. This allows me to tailor my recruitment strategy to attract candidates with the right expertise in AI technologies.

To summarize, data plays a critical role in my decision-making process as a Talent Acquisition Specialist specializing in top-tier IT companies. It helps me identify in-demand skills, evaluate recruitment strategies, screen and select candidates, assess candidate performance, and optimize my overall talent acquisition strategy.

Diversity and Inclusion in Recruitment

Diversity and inclusion in recruitment refers to the practice of actively seeking and hiring candidates from a wide range of backgrounds, experiences, and perspectives, while also fostering an inclusive and equitable work environment.

By prioritizing diversity and inclusion in recruitment, companies can benefit from increased innovation, improved decision-making, better problem-solving, and enhanced employee engagement.

Some key strategies for promoting diversity and inclusion in recruitment include:

1. Creating inclusive job descriptions and advertisements that attract candidates from diverse backgrounds.

2. Using diverse recruitment channels to reach a wider pool of candidates, such as job boards, social media platforms, and professional networking events.

3. Implementing blind resume screening processes to reduce unconscious bias and focus solely on qualifications and experience.

4. Conducting structured interviews that assess candidates based on objective criteria and skills rather than personal characteristics.

5. Establishing diverse interview panels that represent different perspectives and backgrounds to ensure a fair and unbiased evaluation of candidates.

6. Offering diversity and inclusion training to recruiters and hiring managers to raise awareness and promote equitable hiring practices.

Real-world examples of companies that prioritize diversity and inclusion in recruitment include:

• Google: The tech giant has implemented various initiatives to increase diversity in its workforce, such as unconscious bias training and diverse interview panels.

• Salesforce: The company has set diversity goals and implemented programs to attract and retain diverse talent, such as mentorship programs and employee resource groups.

• Airbnb: The company has implemented the 'Open Doors' policy, which ensures that underrepresented candidates are considered for every open position.

• Microsoft: The company has a dedicated diversity and inclusion team that focuses on creating an inclusive work environment and implementing inclusive hiring practices.

In summary, diversity and inclusion in recruitment is crucial for organizations looking to build a diverse and inclusive workforce. By implementing strategies that prioritize diversity and inclusion, companies can attract top talent from diverse backgrounds and benefit from the numerous advantages that diversity brings.

How do you incorporate diversity and inclusion in your recruitment efforts?

Answer

To incorporate diversity and inclusion in my recruitment efforts as a Talent Acquisition Specialist specializing in top-tier IT companies, I follow a comprehensive approach that includes the following steps:

1. Educate myself and the hiring team: I make sure that I am aware of the importance of diversity and inclusion in the workplace and stay updated on the latest trends and best practices. I also educate the hiring team about the benefits of diversity and inclusion to foster a shared understanding and commitment.

2. Review job descriptions and requirements: I carefully review job descriptions and requirements to eliminate any biased language or unnecessary qualifications that may exclude diverse candidates. I focus on the core skills and competencies required for the role, rather than relying on specific degrees or certifications.

3. Diverse sourcing strategies: I actively implement diverse sourcing strategies to attract candidates from different backgrounds. This includes leveraging diverse job boards, attending industry-specific events targeted at underrepresented groups, partnering with diversity-focused organizations, and utilizing social media platforms to reach a wider audience.

4. Unbiased screening and selection process: I ensure that the screening and selection process is unbiased and free from discrimination. This involves using structured interview questions that are relevant to the role, conducting blind resume reviews to

eliminate unconscious bias, and involving a diverse panel of interviewers to assess candidates objectively.

5. Building diverse interview panels: I make an effort to build diverse interview panels that represent different perspectives and backgrounds. This helps in reducing bias and provides a fair evaluation of candidates.

6. Diversity and inclusion training: I provide diversity and inclusion training to the hiring team to equip them with the necessary skills and knowledge to assess candidates objectively and fairly.

7. Promoting diversity and inclusion in employer branding: I emphasize diversity and inclusion in the employer branding efforts to attract a diverse pool of candidates. This includes showcasing diverse employee stories, highlighting inclusive policies and initiatives, and participating in diversity and inclusion-focused events.

8. Tracking and measuring diversity metrics: I track and analyze diversity metrics to measure the effectiveness of our recruitment efforts. This helps in identifying any gaps or areas of improvement and allows us to continuously refine our strategies.

By following this approach, I aim to create a diverse and inclusive workforce that not only reflects the values of the organization but also brings a wide range of perspectives and experiences to drive innovation and success.

Discuss your experience with diverse candidate sourcing?

Answer

In my role as a Talent Acquisition Specialist specializing in top-tier IT companies, I have gained extensive experience in diverse candidate sourcing. Here are some key points about my experience:

• I have developed and implemented strategies to attract candidates from diverse backgrounds, including underrepresented groups such as women, minority communities, and people with disabilities. This includes partnering with organizations and communities that focus on diversity and inclusion.

• I have utilized various sourcing channels, including job boards, social media platforms, professional networks, and industry-specific forums, to reach out to diverse candidates. For example, I have actively engaged with online communities and groups that cater to specific demographics, such as women in tech or minority professionals in IT.

• I have worked closely with hiring managers and team leaders to understand the specific requirements and expectations for each position. This helps me tailor my sourcing efforts to attract candidates with diverse skills, experiences, and backgrounds that align with the company's needs.

• I have leveraged data and analytics to identify patterns and trends in candidate sourcing. This helps me make data-driven decisions on which sourcing channels and strategies are most effective in attracting diverse candidates.

• I have also implemented diversity-focused initiatives, such as hosting diversity recruiting events, attending career fairs at universities with diverse student populations, and partnering with diversity-focused organizations to promote job opportunities to their members.

Overall, my experience with diverse candidate sourcing has been focused on creating an inclusive and equitable hiring process that attracts candidates from all backgrounds and experiences. I believe in the value of diversity in driving innovation and success, and I am committed to ensuring that top-tier IT companies have access to a diverse pool of talent.

What strategies do you use to reduce bias in the recruitment process?

Answer

Use blind screening techniques: Remove names, genders, and other identifying information from resumes during the initial screening process to focus solely on the qualifications and experience of the candidates.

Implement structured interviews: Create a standardized set of interview questions and evaluation criteria that are used for all candidates to ensure fairness and consistency.

Train interviewers on unconscious bias: Provide training to interviewers to raise awareness of unconscious biases and teach them how to avoid making biased decisions.

Diversify the recruitment team: Ensure that the team involved in the recruitment process is diverse in terms of gender, race, and background to bring different perspectives and reduce bias.

Set clear criteria for evaluation: Clearly define the skills, qualifications, and experience required for the role and use these criteria as the basis for evaluating candidates.

Use technology tools: Leverage technology tools such as applicant tracking systems and AI-powered software to remove bias from the screening and evaluation process.

Monitor and analyze data: Regularly review recruitment data to identify any patterns of bias and take corrective actions to address them.

Promote diversity and inclusion: Actively promote diversity and inclusion within the organization to create an inclusive culture that values and supports the hiring of a diverse workforce.

How do you ensure a diverse slate of candidates for each role?

Answer

To ensure a diverse slate of candidates for each role, a Talent Acquisition Specialist specializing in top-tier IT companies can employ the following strategies:

1. Develop a comprehensive job description that is inclusive and appealing to a wide range of candidates. This means using gender-neutral language, avoiding discriminatory requirements, and emphasizing the company's commitment to diversity and inclusion.

2. Expand the talent pool by proactively sourcing candidates from a variety of channels. This can include attending industry events, leveraging professional networks, partnering with diversity-focused organizations, and utilizing online job boards and social media platforms.

3. Use blind screening techniques to eliminate unconscious bias during the initial screening process. This can involve removing

personally identifiable information from resumes and focusing solely on qualifications and skills.

4. Implement structured interview processes that are standardized and consistent for all candidates. This helps to ensure fair and objective evaluations based on merit rather than personal preferences or biases.

5. Offer diversity training to hiring managers and interviewers to raise awareness of unconscious biases and promote inclusive hiring practices. This can help to ensure that all candidates are evaluated fairly and based on their qualifications.

6. Set diversity goals and track progress to measure the effectiveness of diversity initiatives. Regularly reviewing and analyzing recruitment data can provide insights into areas of improvement and help identify any potential biases or barriers in the hiring process.

7. Develop partnerships with educational institutions and organizations that promote diversity in the IT industry. This can include offering internships, mentorship programs, and scholarships to underrepresented groups.

8. Foster an inclusive company culture that values diversity and celebrates differences. This can be achieved through employee resource groups, diversity and inclusion committees, and initiatives that promote a sense of belonging for all employees.

9. Continuously evaluate and refine diversity and inclusion strategies to ensure ongoing improvement and adaptation to changing demographics and industry trends.

By implementing these strategies, a Talent Acquisition Specialist can ensure a diverse slate of candidates for each role, ultimately leading to a more inclusive and innovative workforce.

Talent Acquisition Technology

Talent Acquisition Technology refers to the tools and software used by Talent Acquisition Specialists to streamline and improve the recruitment process.

It encompasses a wide range of technologies, including applicant tracking systems (ATS), candidate relationship management (CRM) systems, video interviewing platforms, job boards, social media platforms, and data analytics software.

These technologies help Talent Acquisition Specialists to attract, assess, and hire top talent more efficiently and effectively.

For example, an ATS allows recruiters to post job openings, track applications, and manage candidate data in a centralized database. This helps them to easily search and filter candidates based on specific criteria, schedule interviews, and collaborate with hiring managers.

CRM systems enable recruiters to build and maintain relationships with potential candidates, track their interactions, and nurture them for future opportunities.

Video interviewing platforms facilitate remote interviews, saving time and resources by eliminating the need for in-person meetings.

Job boards and social media platforms provide a wide reach to attract candidates and promote job openings.

Data analytics software allows Talent Acquisition Specialists to analyze recruitment data, identify trends, and make data-driven decisions to improve the hiring process.

In summary, Talent Acquisition Technology plays a vital role in helping Talent Acquisition Specialists streamline their recruitment process, attract top talent, and make more informed hiring decisions.

What applicant tracking systems have you used, and how do you leverage them?

Answer

I have used several applicant tracking systems (ATS) throughout my career as a Talent Acquisition Specialist specializing in top-tier IT companies. Some of the ATS platforms I have experience with include: (select the ones which you have experience in)

- BambooHR
- BreezyHR
- iCIMS
- SmartRecruiters
- Freshteam by Freshworks
- JazzHR
- Rippling
- Greenhouse
- Zoho Recruit
- Bullhorn
- IBM Kenexa BrassRing
- Jobvite
- Oracle Taleo

Each ATS has its own unique features and functionalities, but the core purpose remains the same: to streamline the hiring process and manage candidate applications efficiently.

Here is how I leverage these ATS platforms to enhance my talent acquisition efforts:

1. Job Posting and Distribution: I utilize the ATS to post job openings on various job boards and social media platforms. This helps in attracting a wider pool of candidates and increases the visibility of the job opportunities.

2. Resume Screening and Filtering: The ATS allows me to automate the initial screening process by setting specific criteria and keywords. This helps in filtering out irrelevant resumes and shortlisting qualified candidates for further evaluation.

3. Candidate Database Management: The ATS helps in maintaining a centralized database of candidate profiles, including their resumes, contact information, and interview notes. This enables easy access and retrieval of candidate information when needed.

4. Collaboration and Communication: ATS platforms provide tools for collaboration and communication within the hiring team. This includes features like interview scheduling, feedback sharing, and candidate status updates. These functionalities facilitate seamless coordination and enhance the overall hiring experience.

5. Reporting and Analytics: I leverage the reporting and analytics capabilities of ATS platforms to track key hiring metrics, such as

time-to-fill, source effectiveness, and candidate conversion rates. This data helps in identifying areas for improvement and making data-driven hiring decisions.

By effectively utilizing these applicant tracking systems, I have been able to streamline the recruitment process, improve candidate quality, and reduce time-to-hire.

Discuss your experience with recruitment marketing tools?

Answer

I have extensive experience in using various recruitment marketing tools to attract top-tier IT talent for leading companies.

Some of the recruitment marketing tools I have used include:

• Applicant tracking systems (ATS): These tools are essential for managing the entire recruitment process, from posting job listings to tracking applicant progress and communicating with candidates. I have used popular ATS software like Greenhouse and Workable to streamline and automate our recruitment workflows.

• Social media platforms: I have leveraged platforms like LinkedIn, Facebook, and Twitter to promote job openings and engage with potential candidates. By creating targeted campaigns and using relevant hashtags, I have been able to reach a wide pool of qualified candidates.

• Job boards: I have utilized popular job boards like Indeed, Monster, and Dice to post job listings and attract a diverse range of candidates. These platforms offer advanced search and filtering options, allowing recruiters to find candidates with specific skills and experience.

• Employee referral programs: I have implemented employee referral programs to tap into our existing network and encourage employees to refer qualified candidates. This has proven to be an effective way to source high-quality talent, as referrals often come with a pre-established trust and understanding of our company culture.

• Talent relationship management (TRM) systems: TRM systems help recruiters build and maintain relationships with potential candidates, even if they are not actively looking for a job. I have used tools like SmashFly and Avature to nurture talent pipelines and engage with passive candidates.

These are just a few examples of the recruitment marketing tools I have experience with. I am always eager to explore new tools and technologies that can enhance our talent acquisition strategies.

In summary, my experience with recruitment marketing tools spans applicant tracking systems, social media platforms, job boards, employee referral programs, and talent relationship management systems. By utilizing these tools effectively, I have been able to attract top-tier IT talent for leading companies.

How do you stay updated on emerging technologies in talent acquisition?

Answer

I believe that staying updated on emerging technologies is crucial for a Talent Acquisition Specialist specializing in top-tier IT companies. Here are some ways in which I stay updated:

Networking: I actively participate in industry events, conferences, and meetups to connect with other professionals in the field. This allows me to learn about the latest trends and technologies in talent acquisition.

Online Resources: I regularly follow reputable websites, blogs, and social media accounts that focus on talent acquisition and emerging technologies. These platforms provide insights, case studies, and best practices that help me stay updated.

Professional Development: I invest in continuous learning and professional development courses related to talent acquisition and technology. These courses help me stay updated on the latest tools, platforms, and techniques used in the industry.

Collaboration: I collaborate with colleagues and industry experts to discuss emerging technologies and share knowledge. This collaborative approach enables me to gain insights from different perspectives and stay updated on the latest trends.

Real-World Projects: I actively engage in real-world projects and experiments to gain hands-on experience with emerging technologies. This practical experience helps me understand the challenges and opportunities associated with these technologies.

Summary: To stay updated on emerging technologies in talent acquisition, I network with industry professionals, follow online resources, invest in professional development, collaborate with colleagues, and engage in real-world projects.

What role does artificial intelligence play in your recruitment process?

Answer

Artificial intelligence (AI) plays a crucial role in our recruitment process as a Talent Acquisition Specialist specializing in top-tier IT companies.

AI helps us streamline and automate various aspects of the recruitment process, making it more efficient and effective. Here are some key roles AI plays in our recruitment process:

• Resume screening: AI-powered algorithms can analyze resumes and identify top candidates based on specific criteria. This saves time and ensures that only the most qualified candidates are considered for further evaluation.

• Candidate sourcing: AI tools can search through various online platforms, social media, and job boards to find potential candidates with the right skills and qualifications. This helps us reach a larger pool of candidates and increases the chances of finding the best fit for the job.

• Skill assessment: AI-based assessments can evaluate candidates' skills and knowledge in specific areas, providing objective and standardized results. This helps us identify candidates with the required expertise and ensures fair evaluation throughout the recruitment process.

• Chatbot assistance: AI-powered chatbots can interact with candidates, providing them with information about job openings, answering frequently asked questions, and even conducting initial screenings. This improves the candidate experience and reduces the workload for recruiters.

• Predictive analytics: AI algorithms can analyze large volumes of data to identify patterns and make predictions about candidate success. This helps us make data-driven decisions and improve the accuracy of our hiring process.

• Bias reduction: AI can help minimize unconscious bias in the recruitment process by focusing on objective criteria and removing personal information that may lead to bias. This promotes fairness and diversity in our hiring practices.

Overall, AI enhances our recruitment process by saving time, expanding candidate reach, improving assessment accuracy, enhancing candidate experience, enabling data-driven decisions, and promoting fairness and diversity.

Candidate Experience

Candidate experience refers to the overall experience that a candidate has during the recruitment process.

It includes every interaction and touchpoint that a candidate has with the company, from the initial application to the final decision.

A positive candidate experience can help to attract top talent and build a strong employer brand, while a negative experience can harm the company's reputation and make it difficult to attract quality candidates.

Here are some key aspects of candidate experience:

• Clear communication: Providing clear and timely communication to candidates throughout the process, including updates on the status of their application and next steps.

• Transparent process: Being transparent about the recruitment process, including the timeline, the selection criteria, and the decision-making process.

• Respectful treatment: Treating candidates with respect and professionalism, providing a positive and welcoming experience.

• Smooth application process: Ensuring that the application process is user-friendly and easy to navigate, with clear instructions and minimal barriers.

• Engaging interviews: Conducting interviews that are well-prepared, relevant to the role, and give candidates the opportunity to showcase their skills and experience.

• Timely feedback: Providing timely and constructive feedback to candidates, whether they are successful or not.

A good candidate experience can also extend beyond the recruitment process itself. For example, it may include onboarding and integration into the company culture.

Overall, creating a positive candidate experience requires a focus on clear communication, transparency, respect, and engagement throughout the recruitment process.

How do you ensure a positive and respectful candidate experience?

Answer

To ensure a positive and respectful candidate experience as a Talent Acquisition Specialist specializing in top-tier IT companies, the following strategies can be implemented:

1. Clear and transparent communication: Communicate the hiring process, job requirements, and expectations clearly and transparently with candidates. Provide regular updates and feedback throughout the process to keep candidates informed and engaged.

2. Respectful and prompt communication: Respond to candidate inquiries and applications promptly and respectfully. Treat candidates with professionalism and courtesy at all times.

3. Personalized approach: Tailor the candidate experience to each individual by understanding their unique needs and preferences. For example, some candidates may prefer email communication while others may prefer phone calls or video interviews. Adapting to their preferred communication style can make the experience more positive and respectful.

4. Provide a realistic job preview: Give candidates a clear understanding of the job responsibilities, challenges, and work environment. This helps manage expectations and ensures that candidates have a realistic view of the role before accepting an offer.

5. Engage candidates throughout the process: Keep candidates engaged and excited about the opportunity by involving them in the hiring process. This can include inviting them to meet the team, participate in a skills assessment, or attend a company event.

6. Timely and constructive feedback: Provide timely and constructive feedback to candidates after interviews or assessments. This helps candidates understand their strengths and areas for improvement, and also shows respect for their time and effort in the process.

7. Continuous improvement: Regularly seek feedback from candidates to identify areas for improvement in the candidate experience. This can be done through surveys, interviews, or informal conversations. Use this feedback to make necessary changes and enhancements to the hiring process.

Real-world example: In a recent hiring process for a top-tier IT company, we ensured a positive and respectful candidate experience by implementing these strategies. We provided clear communication about the hiring process, promptly responded to candidate inquiries, and personalized the experience based on their preferences. We also gave candidates a realistic job preview and engaged them throughout the process by involving them in team meetings and a skills assessment. After each stage, we provided constructive feedback to candidates and continuously sought their input to improve the experience.

Discuss your approach to providing constructive feedback to candidates?

Answer

I believe in providing constructive feedback to candidates to help them improve and grow in their careers. My approach to providing feedback includes:

1. Being specific: I make sure to provide specific feedback to candidates, highlighting both their strengths and areas for improvement. This allows them to have a clear understanding of their performance and areas they can work on.

For example, if a candidate did well in the technical interview but struggled with communication skills, I would provide feedback on their technical knowledge and suggest ways they can improve their communication skills.

2. Using real-world examples: I find that using real-world examples helps candidates better understand the feedback and how they can apply it in their future interviews or work. I provide specific examples of situations where they excelled or could have improved.

For instance, if a candidate struggled with problem-solving during a coding exercise, I would provide an example of a similar problem they could have approached differently.

3. Encouraging self-reflection: I believe in empowering candidates to take ownership of their growth and development. I encourage them to reflect on their performance and identify areas they can work on.

To facilitate self-reflection, I often ask candidates questions like 'What do you think went well in this interview?' or 'What areas would you like to improve upon?' This helps them gain insights and take proactive steps towards improvement.

4. Providing actionable suggestions: Along with feedback, I provide actionable suggestions to candidates on how they can improve. These suggestions are tailored to their specific areas of improvement and provide concrete steps they can take.

For example, if a candidate needs to improve their problem-solving skills, I might suggest practicing coding problems regularly or seeking additional training resources.

In summary, my approach to providing constructive feedback to candidates involves being specific, using real-world examples, encouraging self-reflection, and providing actionable suggestions. By following this approach, I aim to help candidates grow and improve in their careers.

What steps do you take to minimize candidate drop-off during the recruitment process?

Answer

1. Streamline the application process: Simplify the application process by minimizing the number of steps and fields required. Make sure the application form is user-friendly and mobile-responsive, as many candidates prefer to apply through their mobile devices. Avoid asking for redundant information that can be gathered later in the process.

2. Clear and realistic job descriptions: Provide clear and concise job descriptions that accurately reflect the role and its requirements. Avoid using jargon or vague terms that may confuse or discourage potential candidates. Use real-world examples or success stories to highlight the impact and growth opportunities available in the role.

3. Regular communication: Maintain consistent communication with candidates throughout the recruitment process. Provide timely updates on the status of their application, and be transparent about the timeline and next steps. This helps to keep candidates engaged and minimizes the chances of them dropping off due to uncertainty or lack of information.

4. Engaging interviews: Conduct structured and engaging interviews that allow candidates to showcase their skills and qualifications. Use behavioral-based questions to assess their past experiences and problem-solving abilities. Provide a positive and welcoming interview experience to leave a lasting impression and keep candidates interested in the opportunity.

5. Personalized candidate experience: Tailor the recruitment process to each candidate's needs and preferences. Offer flexibility in interview scheduling, accommodate reasonable requests, and provide personalized feedback based on their performance. This personalized approach makes candidates feel valued and increases their commitment to the process.

6. Efficient decision-making: Minimize delays in the decision-making process by establishing clear evaluation criteria and involving all relevant stakeholders in the hiring decision. Communicate the decision promptly to the candidate and provide constructive feedback, even if they are not selected. This helps to maintain a positive employer brand and keeps candidates engaged for future opportunities.

7. Continuous improvement: Regularly review and analyze the recruitment process to identify areas for improvement. Collect feedback from candidates and hiring managers to understand their experience and identify any pain points. Use this feedback to refine the process and make it more efficient and candidate-friendly.

How do you handle candidate dissatisfaction or negative feedback?

Answer
1. Listen actively: When a candidate expresses dissatisfaction or provides negative feedback, it is important to actively listen to their concerns and understand their perspective. Give them your full attention and show empathy towards their feelings.

2. Acknowledge their concerns: Once you have listened to the candidate, acknowledge their concerns and let them know that you understand their frustration. This helps in building trust and showing that you value their feedback.

3. Apologize if necessary: If the candidate has experienced a negative situation or has been treated poorly, apologize for the inconvenience caused. This shows that you take responsibility for any mistakes or shortcomings.

4. Offer a solution: After acknowledging their concerns, offer a solution or provide options to address the issue. This can include reevaluating their application, connecting them with a different opportunity, or providing additional support or information.

5. Follow up: After implementing a solution or taking necessary actions, follow up with the candidate to ensure their satisfaction and to address any further concerns they may have. This step helps in closing the loop and maintaining a positive relationship with the candidate.

Legal and Compliance

As a Talent Acquisition Specialist specializing in top-tier IT companies, it is important to have a strong understanding of legal and compliance requirements in the recruiting process.

Some key legal and compliance considerations include:
• Equal Employment Opportunity (EEO) laws: It is essential to ensure that the recruitment process is fair and unbiased, and that candidates are not discriminated against based on factors such as race, gender, age, disability, or religion. This includes following proper guidelines for job advertisements, candidate screening, interviewing, and selection processes.
• Privacy laws: Talent acquisition specialists must handle candidate data and personal information in accordance with privacy laws, such as the General Data Protection Regulation (GDPR) in Europe. This includes obtaining appropriate consent from candidates, securely storing and managing candidate data, and ensuring data protection measures are in place.
• Employment contracts: Talent acquisition specialists should have a good understanding of employment contract laws and ensure that job offers and contracts comply with relevant regulations. This includes understanding specific clauses, such as non-compete agreements or intellectual property rights.
• Immigration laws: If recruiting candidates from different countries, talent acquisition specialists need to be aware of immigration laws and visa requirements. This includes ensuring that candidates have the legal right to work in the country where the job is located and following the necessary procedures for work permits or visas.
• Anti-discrimination laws: Talent acquisition specialists must be knowledgeable about laws that prohibit discrimination in the workplace, such as the Americans with Disabilities Act (ADA) or the Age Discrimination in Employment Act (ADEA). This includes making reasonable accommodations for candidates with disabilities during the recruitment process.

Real-world example:
For example, let's say you are recruiting for a top-tier IT company and you receive a resume from a highly qualified candidate.

However, during the interview, the candidate discloses that they have a disability. As a talent acquisition specialist, you must ensure that you follow the necessary steps to provide reasonable accommodations for the candidate during the interview process, such as arranging for an accessible interview location or providing assistive technology if needed. This is to ensure compliance with anti-discrimination laws and to give the candidate an equal opportunity to showcase their skills and qualifications.

Summary:
Legal and compliance considerations in talent acquisition for top-tier IT companies include equal employment opportunity laws, privacy laws, employment contract laws, immigration laws, and anti-discrimination laws. Talent acquisition specialists must ensure fairness, proper handling of candidate data, compliance with employment contracts, adherence to immigration requirements, and making reasonable accommodations for candidates with disabilities.

How do you ensure compliance with labor laws and regulations in recruitment?

Answer
To ensure compliance with labor laws and regulations in recruitment, Talent Acquisition Specialists specializing in top-tier IT companies can follow these steps:
• Familiarize themselves with relevant labor laws and regulations: Talent Acquisition Specialists need to have a thorough understanding of the labor laws and regulations that apply to their recruitment activities. This includes laws related to equal employment opportunity, minimum wage, working hours, and employment contracts.
• Stay updated with changes in labor laws: Labor laws and regulations can change over time, so it is important for Talent Acquisition Specialists to stay updated with any changes or updates in the laws that may affect their recruitment practices. This can be done through regular monitoring of government websites, attending seminars or workshops on labor laws, or consulting with legal experts.

• Develop and implement recruitment policies and procedures: Talent Acquisition Specialists need to develop and implement recruitment policies and procedures that are compliant with labor laws and regulations. These policies and procedures should outline the steps and processes that will be followed during the recruitment process, ensuring fair and equal treatment of all applicants.

• Conduct thorough background checks: Talent Acquisition Specialists should conduct thorough background checks on potential candidates to ensure compliance with labor laws and regulations. This includes verifying employment history, checking references, and conducting criminal background checks if necessary. These checks help to ensure that the candidate is suitable for the position and meets the requirements set by the labor laws.

• Maintain accurate and up-to-date records: Talent Acquisition Specialists should maintain accurate and up-to-date records of all recruitment activities and documentation. This includes job postings, resumes, interview notes, reference checks, and any other relevant documents. These records serve as evidence of compliance with labor laws and can be used for audit purposes if required.

• Train and educate hiring managers: Talent Acquisition Specialists should provide training and education to hiring managers on labor laws and regulations related to recruitment. This helps to ensure that hiring managers are aware of their responsibilities and obligations under the law, and that they follow the proper procedures during the recruitment process.

• Seek legal advice if needed: In case of any doubts or uncertainties regarding labor laws and regulations, Talent Acquisition Specialists should seek legal advice from experts in labor law. This can help to clarify any issues and ensure compliance with the law.

By following these steps, Talent Acquisition Specialists can ensure compliance with labor laws and regulations in recruitment, reducing the risk of legal issues and creating a fair and transparent recruitment process.

Discuss your experience with handling sensitive information in recruitment?

Answer

I have extensive experience in handling sensitive information in recruitment, particularly in top-tier IT companies. Here are some key points about my experience:

I understand the importance of confidentiality and data security in the recruitment process, especially when dealing with sensitive information such as candidates' personal details, employment history, and salary expectations.

I have implemented strict protocols and procedures to ensure the safe handling of sensitive information. This includes using secure file-sharing platforms, password-protecting documents, and limiting access to authorized personnel only.

I have worked with cross-functional teams, including legal and compliance, to establish data protection policies and ensure compliance with privacy regulations such as GDPR and CCPA.

I have conducted training sessions for staff members involved in the recruitment process to educate them about the importance of data security and confidentiality. This helps in creating awareness among team members and reduces the risk of data breaches.

In my previous role as a Talent Acquisition Specialist at XYZ IT Solutions, I was responsible for managing a large volume of sensitive candidate information. I ensured that all data was stored securely and only accessed by authorized individuals.

One real-world example of how I handled sensitive information is when I had to conduct background checks on potential candidates. I worked closely with a third-party background screening company to ensure that the information gathered was accurate and confidential. I maintained strict confidentiality throughout the process and only shared the results with relevant stakeholders.

Another example is when I had to negotiate job offers with candidates. I always ensured that sensitive information such as salary expectations and benefits were handled discreetly and only shared with the necessary decision-makers.

To summarize, my experience with handling sensitive information in recruitment includes implementing strict protocols, collaborating with cross-functional teams, conducting training sessions, and maintaining confidentiality throughout the process. I have successfully managed sensitive data in my previous roles and understand the importance of data security in recruitment.

What measures do you take to promote fair and ethical recruitment practices?

Answer

Implementing a comprehensive diversity and inclusion strategy that ensures equal opportunities for all candidates.

Using blind screening techniques to eliminate bias and focus solely on skills and qualifications.

Establishing clear job requirements and criteria to avoid any subjective decision-making.

Training hiring managers and interviewers on unconscious bias and fair hiring practices.

Conducting thorough background checks and reference checks to verify candidate information.

Ensuring transparent and timely communication with candidates throughout the recruitment process.

Regularly reviewing and updating recruitment policies and procedures to align with industry best practices and legal requirements.

Collaborating with internal stakeholders to develop and maintain a positive employer brand.

Engaging in partnerships with organizations that promote diversity and inclusion in the IT industry.

Monitoring and analyzing recruitment metrics to identify any potential biases or disparities in the hiring process.

Establishing a feedback mechanism for candidates to provide input on their recruitment experience.

Regularly conducting internal audits to ensure compliance with fair and ethical recruitment practices.

Remote and Hybrid Hiring

Remote and hybrid hiring refers to the process of recruiting and onboarding employees who will work remotely or in a combination of remote and on-site settings. This approach has become increasingly popular, especially in the IT industry, where many companies are embracing remote work and flexible work arrangements. Remote hiring allows companies to tap into a global talent pool and access top talent from anywhere in the world, regardless of geographical constraints. Hybrid hiring combines remote work with occasional on-site work, allowing companies to strike a balance between the benefits of remote work and the advantages of in-person collaboration.

Here are some key considerations and strategies for remote and hybrid hiring:
1. Define the job requirements and skills needed for remote work: Clearly outline the skills and qualifications necessary for successful remote work, such as self-motivation, communication skills, and the ability to work independently.
2. Implement a robust screening and interview process: Use video interviews and remote assessment tools to evaluate candidates' technical skills and cultural fit.
3. Leverage technology for onboarding: Use online platforms and tools to facilitate virtual onboarding, including providing access to necessary software and resources.
4. Establish clear communication channels: Utilize collaboration tools and establish regular check-ins to ensure effective communication and alignment among remote team members.
5. Foster a remote-friendly culture: Create a supportive and inclusive remote work culture by organizing virtual team-building activities, offering flexible work hours, and providing opportunities for professional development.
6. Offer competitive compensation and benefits: Consider the cost of living in different locations and adjust compensation accordingly. Provide benefits that support remote work, such as home office allowances or reimbursement for internet expenses.

7. Monitor and adapt: Continuously monitor the effectiveness of remote and hybrid hiring strategies and make adjustments as needed to optimize the process and support employee success.

Real-world example: Company XYZ is a leading IT company that specializes in remote and hybrid hiring. They have successfully built a global team of top-tier IT professionals who work remotely or in a hybrid arrangement. XYZ has established clear communication channels, implemented a robust screening process, and provides competitive compensation and benefits to attract and retain top talent.

How do you adapt your recruitment strategies for remote or hybrid work environments?

Answer

- Utilize online platforms and tools for job postings and candidate sourcing
- Leverage video conferencing and virtual interview techniques
- Adjust the evaluation criteria to focus more on remote work skills and qualities
- Implement remote onboarding processes and training programs
- Establish clear communication channels and expectations for remote or hybrid teams
- Offer flexible work arrangements to attract and retain remote talent
- Provide resources and support for remote employees to thrive in their roles
- Regularly assess and refine recruitment strategies based on feedback and data

Discuss your experience with virtual onboarding and remote hiring processes?

Answer

I have extensive experience in virtual onboarding and remote hiring processes, particularly in the IT industry. During my time as a Talent Acquisition Specialist at a top-tier IT company, I have successfully onboarded and hired numerous candidates remotely.

Here are some key points about my experience:
• Developed and implemented a virtual onboarding program that streamlined the process and ensured new hires had a smooth transition into the company.
• Created comprehensive onboarding materials, including video tutorials, documentation, and online training modules, to help new hires understand company policies, procedures, and culture.
• Conducted virtual orientation sessions to introduce new hires to key team members, provide an overview of the company's mission and values, and answer any questions they may have.
• Coordinated with IT and HR departments to ensure new hires had the necessary equipment, software, and access to company systems and tools for remote work.
• Utilized video conferencing platforms, such as Zoom and Microsoft Teams, to conduct remote interviews and assessments with candidates.
• Collaborated with hiring managers and cross-functional teams to define job requirements, evaluate candidates, and make data-driven hiring decisions.
In terms of remote hiring processes, I have experience in the following:
• Leveraging online job boards, professional networking platforms, and social media to source and attract top talent.
• Conducting virtual interviews, including technical assessments, behavioral interviews, and cultural fit evaluations.
• Coordinating and scheduling interviews with multiple stakeholders across different time zones.

• Using applicant tracking systems (ATS) to manage the hiring pipeline, track candidate progress, and ensure a smooth and efficient process.

Overall, my experience with virtual onboarding and remote hiring processes has allowed me to effectively adapt to the challenges of remote work and successfully onboard and hire top talent for top-tier IT companies.

What challenges do you anticipate in remote recruitment, and how do you address them?

Answer

The challenges in remote recruitment include:

• Limited access to candidates: Remote recruitment may limit access to a diverse pool of candidates, especially those who do not have access to technology or reliable internet connection. To address this, we can use alternative methods such as phone interviews or partnering with local recruitment agencies to reach a wider audience.

• Communication barriers: Remote recruitment can lead to communication challenges, as it may be difficult to convey tone or build rapport over virtual platforms. To overcome this, we can conduct video interviews to establish a more personal connection, use clear and concise language in written communications, and provide detailed job descriptions to set expectations.

• Technical difficulties: Remote recruitment relies heavily on technology, and technical difficulties can arise during the hiring process. To mitigate this, we can conduct test runs of virtual interviews or assessments, provide technical support to candidates if needed, and have backup plans in case of any technological issues.

• Onboarding and integration: Remote recruitment may pose challenges in onboarding and integrating new hires into the company culture. To address this, we can provide comprehensive onboarding materials, assign mentors or buddies to new hires for guidance and support, and organize virtual team-building activities to foster a sense of belonging.

• Time zone differences: Remote recruitment may involve dealing with candidates from different time zones, which can make scheduling interviews or coordinating communication challenging. To tackle this, we can offer flexible interview timings, use scheduling tools to find mutually convenient time slots, and be mindful of time zone differences when setting expectations.

In summary, the challenges in remote recruitment can be overcome by leveraging alternative methods, improving communication strategies, being prepared for technical difficulties, implementing effective onboarding processes, and being mindful of time zone differences.

How do you ensure a sense of connection and belonging for remote hires?

Answer

Establish regular communication channels: Set up regular check-ins and team meetings to foster communication and collaboration among remote hires. This can be done through video conferences, instant messaging platforms, or project management tools.

Facilitate virtual team-building activities: Organize virtual team-building activities to promote a sense of connection and camaraderie among remote hires. This can include virtual happy hours, online games, or virtual team-building exercises.

Provide clear expectations and goals: Clearly communicate expectations and goals to remote hires to ensure they feel connected to the overall team objectives. This can be done through regular team meetings or individual check-ins.

Encourage informal conversations: Create opportunities for remote hires to engage in informal conversations with their colleagues. This can be done through dedicated chat channels or virtual coffee breaks.

Recognize and celebrate achievements: Acknowledge and celebrate the achievements of remote hires to make them feel valued and included. This can be done through public recognition or virtual celebrations.

Summary: To ensure a sense of connection and belonging for remote hires, it is important to establish regular communication channels, facilitate virtual team-building activities, provide clear expectations and goals, encourage informal conversations, and recognize and celebrate achievements.

Continuous Learning and Professional Development

Continuous learning and professional development are crucial for a Talent Acquisition Specialist specializing in top-tier IT companies. It is necessary to stay updated with the latest trends, technologies, and best practices in the IT industry to attract and recruit top talent.

Here are some key points to consider:

• **Staying informed about the latest IT trends and technologies:** As a Talent Acquisition Specialist, it is important to keep up with the rapidly evolving IT landscape. This includes staying updated on emerging technologies, programming languages, cloud computing, artificial intelligence, cybersecurity, and other relevant areas. By staying informed, you can better understand the skills and expertise required for various IT roles and attract candidates with the right qualifications.

• **Participating in industry conferences and events:** Attending conferences and events focused on IT and talent acquisition can provide valuable insights and networking opportunities. These events often feature thought leaders, industry experts, and successful professionals who can share their experiences and knowledge. By actively participating in such events, you can expand your professional network and gain new perspectives on talent acquisition strategies.

• **Engaging in online learning platforms and courses:** Online learning platforms like Udemy, Coursera, and LinkedIn Learning offer a wide range of courses and certifications related to IT and talent acquisition. These platforms provide flexible learning options, allowing you to enhance your skills at your own pace. By completing relevant courses and acquiring certifications, you can demonstrate your commitment to continuous learning and professional development.

• **Building relationships with IT professionals and industry experts:** Developing strong relationships with IT professionals and industry experts can be immensely beneficial for a Talent Acquisition Specialist. By networking with professionals in the IT industry, you can gain insights into the latest trends, job market dynamics, and hiring strategies. These relationships can also help you identify potential candidates and build trust with top-tier IT professionals.

• **Implementing feedback and continuous improvement:** Continuous learning and professional development involve being open to feedback and constantly seeking ways to improve. Actively seeking feedback from candidates, hiring managers, and colleagues can help you identify areas for improvement and refine your talent acquisition strategies.

By implementing feedback and continuously improving your skills, you can become a more effective Talent Acquisition Specialist.

To summarize, continuous learning and professional development are essential for a Talent Acquisition Specialist specializing in top-tier IT companies. Staying informed about the latest IT trends, participating in industry conferences, engaging in online learning, building relationships with IT professionals, and implementing feedback are key strategies to ensure ongoing growth and success in this role.

How do you stay updated on recruitment trends and best practices?

Answer

I stay updated on recruitment trends and best practices through a variety of methods:

• **Attending industry conferences and events:** I make it a point to attend conferences and events specific to talent acquisition and recruitment. These events provide valuable insights into the latest trends, best practices, and innovative strategies in the field.

• **Networking with industry professionals:** I actively engage with other talent acquisition specialists and HR professionals through networking platforms, industry groups, and professional associations. By exchanging ideas and experiences with peers, I gain valuable knowledge about emerging trends and best practices.

• **Continuous learning and professional development:** I regularly invest time in reading industry publications, blogs, and books to stay updated on the latest recruitment trends and best practices. I also participate in webinars, online courses, and workshops to expand my knowledge and skills.

• **Following thought leaders and influencers:** I follow influential thought leaders, industry experts, and recruitment influencers on social media platforms like LinkedIn and Twitter. Their insights, articles, and discussions provide valuable information and help me stay updated on the latest trends and best practices.

• **Leveraging technology and analytics:** I use technology tools and recruitment software to streamline and enhance my recruitment processes. These tools often provide insights into industry trends and best practices through data and analytics.

By combining these methods, I ensure that I stay updated on the latest recruitment trends and best practices, enabling me to effectively attract and hire top-tier talent for IT companies.

Discuss any recruitment-related certifications or professional development?

Answer

There are several recruitment-related certifications and professional development opportunities that can enhance a Talent Acquisition Specialist's skills and knowledge in the field. Some of these include:

Certifications:

• Certified Internet Recruiter (CIR): This certification validates the knowledge and skills needed to effectively source and recruit candidates using online resources.

• Certified Staffing Professional (CSP): This certification focuses on the legal and ethical aspects of staffing and provides a comprehensive understanding of the recruitment process.

• Professional in Human Resources (PHR): This certification is offered by the HR Certification Institute and covers a broad range of HR topics, including recruitment and talent acquisition.

Professional Development Opportunities:

• Attend industry conferences and seminars: These events provide opportunities to learn from experts and network with other professionals in the field.
• Join professional associations: Associations like the Society for Human Resource Management (SHRM) offer resources, training, and networking opportunities for recruiters.
• Take online courses or webinars: There are numerous online platforms and webinars that offer specialized training on recruitment techniques, sourcing strategies, and candidate assessment.

Real-world examples of how these certifications and professional development opportunities can benefit a Talent Acquisition Specialist specializing in top-tier IT companies:
• A Talent Acquisition Specialist who holds a Certified Internet Recruiter (CIR) certification will have a deep understanding of how to effectively leverage online resources and platforms to attract top IT talent.
• Attending industry conferences and seminars focused on IT recruitment can provide insights into the latest trends and best practices in the field.
• Joining a professional association like SHRM can provide access to a network of IT recruiters and opportunities to collaborate and share knowledge.

What role does ongoing learning play in your career as a Talent Acquisition Specialist?

Answer
Ongoing learning plays a crucial role in the career of a Talent Acquisition Specialist. It helps to stay updated with the latest trends and best practices in talent acquisition, which is essential for success in this role.
By continuously learning, a Talent Acquisition Specialist can improve their knowledge and skills in various areas, such as sourcing strategies, candidate assessment techniques, employer branding, and diversity and inclusion practices. This enables them to be more effective in attracting and selecting top talent for the organization.

Furthermore, ongoing learning allows a Talent Acquisition Specialist to adapt to changes in the IT industry. Technology advancements, new job roles, and evolving candidate expectations require constant learning to stay relevant. For example, learning about emerging technologies like artificial intelligence or blockchain can help a specialist better understand the skills and qualifications needed for IT roles in top-tier companies.

Real-world examples of ongoing learning in the role of a Talent Acquisition Specialist include:
• Participating in industry conferences and events to learn from experts and network with peers.
• Taking online courses or certifications related to talent acquisition and HR practices.
• Reading industry publications and blogs to stay updated with the latest trends.
• Engaging in continuous professional development through workshops or webinars.
• Collaborating with hiring managers and other HR professionals to learn from their experiences and gain insights into specific IT roles and requirements.
Overall, ongoing learning ensures that a Talent Acquisition Specialist remains competitive, knowledgeable, and capable of attracting and acquiring top IT talent for top-tier companies.

How do you share knowledge and insights with your recruitment team?

Answer
Regular team meetings: I organize regular team meetings where I share important updates, industry trends, and best practices with my recruitment team. This allows us to discuss and brainstorm ideas, address any challenges, and align our strategies.
Training sessions: I conduct training sessions to enhance the skills and knowledge of my recruitment team. These sessions cover topics such as sourcing techniques, interview strategies, and candidate assessment methods. I provide real-world examples and case studies to make the training more practical and relevant.

Documentation: I create and maintain detailed documentation that captures our recruitment processes, tools, and guidelines. This documentation serves as a knowledge base for the team to refer to when needed. It includes step-by-step instructions, templates, and examples to ensure clarity and consistency in our work.

Collaboration platforms: I encourage my team to use collaboration platforms such as Slack or Microsoft Teams to share knowledge and insights in real-time. This allows for quick and easy communication, knowledge exchange, and problem-solving. We can share articles, research papers, and relevant resources to stay updated on industry trends and best practices.

Mentoring and coaching: I provide one-on-one mentoring and coaching sessions to team members to help them develop their skills and expertise. During these sessions, I share my insights, experiences, and lessons learned from working in top-tier IT companies. I also provide feedback and guidance to help them improve their performance.

Summary: In summary, I share knowledge and insights with my recruitment team through regular team meetings, training sessions, documentation, collaboration platforms, and mentoring/coaching sessions. These approaches ensure that the team is well-informed, up-to-date with industry trends, and equipped with the necessary skills to excel in their roles.

Challenges in Recruitment

1. High competition for top talent: The IT industry is highly competitive, and top-tier companies are constantly vying for the same pool of skilled professionals. This means that talent acquisition specialists face challenges in attracting and hiring the best candidates for their organizations.

2. Technical skills shortage: There is often a shortage of candidates with the specific technical skills required for IT roles. This can make it difficult for talent acquisition specialists to find qualified candidates who meet the requirements of the job.

3. Passive candidates: Many top-tier IT professionals are already employed and may not actively be seeking new opportunities. Talent acquisition specialists need to find ways to engage with passive candidates and convince them to consider their organizations.

4. Cultural fit: IT companies often have unique cultures and work environments. Finding candidates who not only have the technical skills but also fit well within the company culture can be a challenge.

5. Speed of hiring: In the IT industry, the demand for talent is high, and companies need to hire quickly to stay competitive. Talent acquisition specialists face the challenge of finding and hiring qualified candidates within tight timelines.

6. Employer branding: Attracting top talent requires a strong employer brand. Talent acquisition specialists need to effectively communicate the value proposition of their organizations and differentiate themselves from competitors.

7. Diversity and inclusion: IT companies recognize the importance of diversity and inclusion in their workforce. Talent acquisition specialists face the challenge of sourcing and attracting candidates from diverse backgrounds to create an inclusive workplace.

8. Retention: Once top talent is hired, talent acquisition specialists need to ensure they are retained. Retention strategies and ongoing engagement are crucial to prevent high turnover rates.

9. Technology advancements: The IT industry is constantly evolving, and talent acquisition specialists need to stay updated on the latest technologies and trends to effectively recruit top IT professionals.

10. Cost of recruitment: Recruitment processes can be costly, especially when hiring for top-tier IT positions. Talent acquisition specialists need to optimize their recruitment strategies to minimize costs while still attracting the best talent.

Share an example of a difficult-to-fill position you successfully recruited for?

Answer

One example of a difficult-to-fill position that I successfully recruited for was a Senior Data Scientist role at a top-tier IT company. The position required a highly specialized skill set and experience in machine learning and data analysis. The challenge was finding candidates who not only had the technical skills but also the ability to apply those skills to real-world business problems. To attract top talent, I used a combination of targeted job postings on industry-specific websites, networking events, and referrals from contacts in the field. I also reached out to professionals on platforms like LinkedIn to directly engage with potential candidates.

During the interview process, I designed a series of technical assessments and case studies to evaluate candidates' abilities to solve complex problems and think critically.

I also conducted thorough reference checks to ensure candidates' experience and expertise matched their resumes.

After an extensive search and evaluation process, I successfully recruited a highly qualified candidate with a proven track record in data science and a strong background in the IT industry. This candidate not only possessed the technical skills required for the position but also demonstrated a deep understanding of the business context in which they would be working. Their expertise and experience have had a significant impact on the company's data analysis capabilities and have contributed to the development of innovative solutions for clients.

Overall, this example showcases my ability to successfully recruit for difficult-to-fill positions by using a combination of targeted sourcing strategies, rigorous evaluation methods, and a deep understanding of the skills and qualifications necessary for the role.

How do you handle situations where there is a lack of interest or qualified candidates?

Answer

- Assess the job description and requirements to ensure they accurately reflect the qualifications and skills needed for the role
- Expand the candidate pool by utilizing various sourcing channels such as job boards, social media platforms, and professional networking sites
- Reach out to passive candidates who may not be actively seeking new opportunities but possess the desired qualifications
- Collaborate with hiring managers and team members to refine the job requirements and identify any potential areas for flexibility or adjustments
- Consider alternative recruitment strategies such as offering referral incentives to current employees or partnering with recruitment agencies specializing in the IT industry
- Review and optimize the recruitment process to ensure it is efficient and effective in attracting qualified candidates
- Develop and maintain relationships with universities, coding bootcamps, and other educational institutions to tap into emerging talent
- Engage in continuous learning and professional development to stay updated on the latest trends and techniques in talent acquisition
- Consider the possibility of upskilling or reskilling existing employees to meet the required qualifications
- Evaluate the employer brand and company reputation to identify any potential areas of improvement that may be hindering candidate interest
- Leverage data and analytics to identify patterns and trends in candidate attraction and engagement, allowing for targeted adjustments and improvements
- Maintain open and transparent communication with candidates throughout the recruitment process, addressing any concerns or questions promptly

- Consider conducting a thorough analysis of the compensation and benefits package to ensure it is competitive and aligned with industry standards
- Provide constructive feedback to candidates who may not have met the qualifications, offering guidance and suggestions for future opportunities
- Consider implementing diversity and inclusion initiatives to attract a wider range of candidates and broaden the talent pool

Summary: When faced with a lack of interest or qualified candidates, it is essential to assess the job requirements, expand the candidate pool, collaborate with hiring managers, optimize the recruitment process, maintain relationships with educational institutions, consider upskilling existing employees, evaluate the employer brand, leverage data and analytics, maintain open communication, analyze the compensation package, provide feedback to candidates, and implement diversity and inclusion initiatives.

What strategies do you use to overcome recruitment challenges in a competitive market?

Answer

1. Developing a strong employer brand: By showcasing the unique aspects of the company culture, benefits, and career opportunities, we can attract top talent and differentiate ourselves from competitors. This can be achieved through creating engaging content on social media, participating in industry events, and leveraging employee testimonials.

2. Building a talent pipeline: By proactively sourcing and nurturing relationships with potential candidates, we can maintain a pool of qualified candidates who are interested in working for our company. This can be done through networking, attending job fairs, and leveraging professional networking platforms like LinkedIn.

3. Streamlining the recruitment process: By optimizing the recruitment process, we can reduce time-to-hire and improve the candidate experience. This can be achieved through automation of

repetitive tasks, using applicant tracking systems, conducting efficient interviews, and providing timely feedback to candidates.

4. Offering competitive compensation and benefits: In a competitive market, it is crucial to offer attractive compensation packages and benefits to attract top talent. This can include competitive salaries, performance-based bonuses, flexible work arrangements, professional development opportunities, and comprehensive health and wellness programs.

5. Leveraging technology and data: By using technology tools and data analytics, we can make informed decisions and optimize our recruitment strategies. This can include using artificial intelligence for resume screening, leveraging data to identify trends and insights, and using predictive analytics to forecast future hiring needs.

6. Engaging passive candidates: In a competitive market, it is important to proactively reach out to passive candidates who may not be actively looking for a job. This can be done through targeted outreach, personalized messaging, and highlighting the unique opportunities our company can offer.

7. Partnering with universities and industry organizations: By establishing partnerships with universities and industry organizations, we can tap into a pool of talented individuals who are interested in the IT field. This can include participating in career fairs, offering internships and co-op programs, and sponsoring industry events.

8. Continuous improvement and learning: In a competitive market, it is important to stay updated with the latest trends and best practices in talent acquisition. This can be achieved through attending industry conferences, participating in webinars and workshops, and continuously seeking feedback from candidates and hiring managers.

How do you approach recruitment for niche or specialized roles?

Answer
- Research and understand the specific requirements of the niche or specialized role.
- Identify the key skills, qualifications, and experience needed for the role.

- Develop a targeted sourcing strategy to find candidates with the desired skills and experience.
- Utilize niche job boards, professional networking sites, and industry-specific communities to identify potential candidates.
- Engage with passive candidates through personalized outreach and networking.
- Screen candidates thoroughly to ensure they meet the required criteria.
- Conduct in-depth interviews to assess the candidate's technical skills, cultural fit, and motivation for the role.
- Collaborate with hiring managers and technical experts to evaluate the candidate's capabilities.
- Present shortlisted candidates to the hiring team with detailed profiles and insights.
- Coordinate and schedule interviews with the hiring team and facilitate the decision-making process.
- Maintain regular communication with candidates throughout the recruitment process.
- Provide a positive candidate experience by keeping them informed and engaged.
- Negotiate job offers and manage the onboarding process for successful candidates.
- Monitor the effectiveness of the recruitment strategy and make adjustments as needed.
- Stay updated with industry trends and developments to proactively identify talent in niche or specialized areas.

Feedback and Improvement

Feedback and improvement are crucial aspects of talent acquisition. Continuous feedback helps in identifying areas of improvement and making necessary adjustments to the recruitment process.

Some ways to gather feedback and improve talent acquisition include:

• Conducting regular surveys or feedback sessions with hiring managers and candidates to understand their experience and identify areas for improvement.

• Analyzing recruitment metrics and data to identify bottlenecks or areas of improvement in the talent acquisition process.

• Seeking input from the HR team and other stakeholders to gather different perspectives and insights on the recruitment process.

• Keeping track of industry trends and best practices in talent acquisition and implementing them in the recruitment process.

• Implementing technology solutions like applicant tracking systems or AI-powered recruitment tools to streamline and improve the efficiency of the talent acquisition process.

Real-world examples of feedback and improvement in talent acquisition include:

• After analyzing recruitment metrics, it is identified that the time-to-hire for IT roles is longer compared to other departments. To address this, the talent acquisition team implements a pre-screening assessment to filter out unqualified candidates early in the process, reducing time-to-hire and improving efficiency.

• Feedback from candidates reveals that the interview process lacks transparency and clear communication. As a result, the talent acquisition team revises the interview process to include regular updates to candidates and clear communication about the next steps.

In summary, feedback and improvement are essential for optimizing the talent acquisition process. By actively seeking feedback, analyzing data, and implementing improvements, talent acquisition specialists can enhance the recruitment experience for both hiring managers and candidates.

How do you seek feedback from candidates and hiring managers to improve the recruitment process?

Answer

- Regularly schedule feedback meetings with candidates and hiring managers to discuss their experience and gather insights.
- Create a survey or feedback form to collect anonymous feedback from candidates and hiring managers. Ask specific questions about their experience with the recruitment process, including areas for improvement.
- Utilize technology platforms that allow candidates and hiring managers to provide feedback directly, such as online review platforms or email surveys.
- Encourage open and honest communication by creating a safe and non-judgmental environment for feedback.
- Actively listen to the feedback provided and take it into consideration when making improvements to the recruitment process.
- Implement changes based on the feedback received to address any pain points or areas of improvement.
- Provide regular updates to candidates and hiring managers on the steps taken to improve the recruitment process based on their feedback.

Discuss a situation where you implemented changes based on feedback?

Answer

In my role as a Talent Acquisition Specialist specializing in top-tier IT companies, I have had several situations where I implemented changes based on feedback. One specific example is when I received feedback from hiring managers that the interview process was too lengthy and cumbersome.

To address this feedback, I conducted a thorough review of the interview process and identified areas where we could streamline and make improvements. I created a timeline of the entire process, from initial screening to final offer, and identified areas where there were unnecessary delays or duplicated efforts.

Based on this analysis, I proposed several changes to the interview process. These changes included:

• Reducing the number of interview rounds from five to three, while still ensuring thorough evaluation of candidates' skills and fit for the role.

• Implementing a structured interview format to ensure consistency and fairness in evaluating candidates.

• Introducing an online assessment tool to assess technical skills early in the process, reducing the need for multiple technical interviews.

• Providing clear communication to candidates about the interview process, including timelines and expectations.

Once these changes were implemented, I closely monitored the impact on the hiring process. I collected feedback from hiring managers and candidates to assess the effectiveness of the changes. The feedback was overwhelmingly positive, with hiring managers reporting a more efficient and effective process, and candidates appreciating the clarity and transparency.

Overall, implementing these changes based on feedback resulted in a more streamlined and effective interview process, reducing the time-to-hire and improving the candidate experience.

What continuous improvement initiatives have you led in recruitment?

Answer
In my role as a Talent Acquisition Specialist specializing in top-tier IT companies, I have led several continuous improvement initiatives in recruitment.

Here are some examples:
• Implemented a new applicant tracking system (ATS) to streamline the recruitment process and improve efficiency. This allowed us to track candidate progress, automate communication, and centralize candidate data.

• Conducted regular audits of our recruitment processes to identify areas for improvement. This involved analyzing metrics such as time-to-hire, cost-per-hire, and candidate satisfaction. Based on the findings, I implemented changes to optimize these metrics.

• Developed and implemented a candidate feedback survey to gather feedback on the recruitment process. This helped us identify pain points and make necessary improvements to enhance the candidate experience.

• Collaborated with hiring managers to establish clear job requirements and selection criteria for each position. This ensured that we were targeting the right candidates and reduced time wasted on reviewing irrelevant resumes.

• Implemented a sourcing strategy focused on building relationships with passive candidates. This involved leveraging social media platforms, attending industry events, and utilizing employee referrals to attract top talent.

• Conducted training sessions for hiring managers on effective interviewing techniques and unconscious bias. This helped improve the quality of candidate assessments and ensured a fair and inclusive hiring process.

• Implemented a diversity and inclusion initiative in recruitment to ensure a diverse candidate pool. This involved partnering with diversity organizations, attending diversity job fairs, and implementing blind resume screening.

• Utilized data analytics to track and measure the success of recruitment initiatives. This allowed us to make data-driven decisions and continuously improve our strategies based on the results.

Overall, my continuous improvement initiatives in recruitment have focused on streamlining processes, enhancing the candidate experience, improving diversity and inclusion, and leveraging data to make informed decisions.

How do you handle constructive criticism in the recruitment process?

Answer

Listen actively: When receiving constructive criticism, it is important to listen attentively and actively. This means giving the person your full attention, maintaining eye contact, and showing genuine interest in what they have to say.

Stay calm and composed: It is natural to feel defensive or upset when receiving criticism, but it is important to remain calm and composed. Take a deep breath, count to ten, and remind yourself that the criticism is meant to help you improve.

Ask clarifying questions: If there is something you do not understand or need more information about, do not hesitate to ask clarifying questions. This shows that you are open to feedback and willing to learn from it.

Reflect on the feedback: After receiving constructive criticism, take some time to reflect on what was said. Consider whether there is any truth to the feedback and how you can use it to improve your recruitment process.

Take action: Once you have processed the feedback, take action to address any areas for improvement. This could involve seeking additional training or resources, changing your approach, or implementing new strategies.

Seek support: If you are struggling to handle the constructive criticism on your own, reach out to a mentor, colleague, or supervisor for support. They can offer guidance and help you navigate the feedback in a constructive way.

Scenario-Based Questions

Scenario-based questions are a common interview technique used to assess a candidate's problem-solving skills, decision-making abilities, and their ability to think on their feet.

These questions provide candidates with a hypothetical situation and ask them how they would respond or handle the situation.

As a Talent Acquisition Specialist specializing in top-tier IT companies, you can use scenario-based questions to assess a candidate's technical skills, their ability to work in a fast-paced and ever-changing environment, and their problem-solving abilities.

Here are some example scenario-based questions you can ask candidates:

• Scenario: A key client is unhappy with the IT services provided by your company. How would you handle this situation?
  • Answer: I would start by scheduling a meeting with the client to understand their concerns and expectations. I would then work closely with our IT team to address the client's concerns and find a solution that meets their needs. Additionally, I would ensure open and transparent communication with the client throughout the process to keep them updated on our progress. This approach demonstrates my ability to handle difficult client situations and work collaboratively with internal teams to find solutions.

• Scenario: You have a tight deadline to hire a skilled IT professional for a critical project. How would you approach this situation?
  • Answer: I would start by reviewing the job requirements and identifying the key skills and experience needed for the project. I would then leverage my network and professional connections to source potential candidates who meet these requirements. Additionally, I would work closely with hiring managers and project stakeholders to understand their specific needs and priorities. By using a targeted and proactive approach, I can ensure that we find the right candidate within the given deadline.

• Scenario: You receive a high volume of applications for an open IT position. How would you efficiently screen and shortlist candidates?
  • Answer: I would start by creating a screening criteria and reviewing resumes against this criteria to identify potential candidates. I would then conduct initial phone screenings to assess candidates' technical skills and cultural fit. Additionally, I would utilize technology and applicant tracking systems to automate the screening process and efficiently manage the high volume of applications. By implementing a systematic and efficient screening process, I can ensure that we identify the most qualified candidates in a timely manner.

These are just a few examples of scenario-based questions that you can use during the interview process. The key is to tailor the questions to the specific role and requirements of the position you are hiring for.

Give an example of when you successfully negotiated a candidate's acceptance of an offer?

Answer

During my time as a Talent Acquisition Specialist at a top-tier IT company, I encountered a situation where a highly sought-after candidate was hesitant to accept our offer due to a competing offer from another company.

I immediately scheduled a call with the candidate to understand their concerns and discuss the details of our offer. I empathized with their situation and highlighted the unique benefits and growth opportunities our company could offer. I also emphasized the company's strong reputation and the potential for long-term career advancement.

To address the candidate's concerns about compensation, I negotiated with our hiring manager to increase the base salary and include additional performance-based bonuses. I presented the revised offer to the candidate and emphasized the improved compensation package, as well as the other benefits we had discussed earlier. I also provided examples of current employees who had joined the company at a similar level and had seen rapid career progression.

After further discussions and negotiations, the candidate expressed their enthusiasm and acceptance of our offer. Throughout the process, I maintained open and transparent communication with the candidate, keeping them updated on the progress of negotiations and addressing any additional concerns they had.

This successful negotiation resulted in the candidate accepting our offer and joining our company.

How do you handle a situation where a key candidate withdraws from the recruitment process?

Answer

Acknowledge the candidate's decision and thank them for their time and consideration.

Ask the candidate for feedback on their reason for withdrawing to gain insights for future improvements.

Ensure the candidate's withdrawal is properly documented in the recruitment system.

Evaluate the impact of the candidate's withdrawal on the overall recruitment process and timeline.

Re-evaluate the remaining candidates to identify potential replacements or adjust the recruitment strategy.

Communicate the candidate's withdrawal to other stakeholders involved in the recruitment process, such as hiring managers or interviewers.

Consider re-engaging with the candidate in the future if they express interest again.

Learn from the situation and identify ways to prevent candidate withdrawals in the future, such as improving the recruitment process or addressing any potential issues that may have led to the withdrawal.

An example of when you had to manage competing offers for the same candidate?

Answer

Yes, I can share an example of when I had to manage competing offers for the same candidate. In my previous role as a Talent Acquisition Specialist at a top-tier IT company, we were recruiting for a highly sought-after software engineer position. We had identified a candidate who had received offers from two other leading IT companies in the market.

To manage the competing offers, I took the following steps:
• I scheduled a meeting with the candidate to discuss their options and understand their preferences and priorities.
• I carefully reviewed the compensation packages and benefits offered by each company to assess their competitiveness.
• I leveraged my network and connections in the industry to gather information about the company culture, work-life balance, growth opportunities, and reputation of each company.
• I presented the candidate with a detailed comparison of the offers, highlighting the key differences and advantages of our company.
• I emphasized our company's strong track record of innovation, the opportunity to work on cutting-edge projects, and the supportive and collaborative work environment.
• I negotiated with the candidate's preferred company to match or improve upon the offers from the other companies.
• I kept open lines of communication with the candidate throughout the process, addressing any concerns or questions they had.

Ultimately, I was successful in convincing the candidate to accept our offer by showcasing the unique benefits and growth opportunities our company had to offer. This experience taught me the importance of understanding a candidate's motivations and priorities, conducting thorough research on competing offers, and effectively communicating the advantages of our company. By managing competing offers strategically, we were able to secure top talent for our organization.

How do you handle a sudden increase in hiring demand for a specific role?

Answer
- Assess the current hiring process and identify areas for improvement
- Collaborate with hiring managers and stakeholders to understand the specific requirements and expectations for the role

- Develop a recruitment strategy to attract and engage qualified candidates
- Utilize various sourcing channels, such as job boards, social media, and professional networks, to reach a larger pool of potential candidates
- Screen resumes and conduct initial interviews to narrow down the candidate pool
- Coordinate and schedule interviews with hiring managers and team members
- Facilitate the decision-making process by gathering feedback from interviewers and providing timely updates to candidates
- Negotiate job offers and manage the onboarding process for successful candidates
- Monitor and track metrics to evaluate the effectiveness of the hiring process and make necessary adjustments
- Provide regular updates and reports to stakeholders on the progress of the hiring efforts

Collaboration with HR and Hiring Teams

As a Talent Acquisition Specialist specializing in top-tier IT companies, collaboration with HR and hiring teams is crucial to successfully recruit and onboard top talent.

Here are some key aspects of collaboration with HR and hiring teams:

• Understanding the hiring needs and requirements: Collaborating with HR and hiring teams involves understanding the specific skills, qualifications, and experience needed for each position. This collaboration helps in creating accurate job descriptions and setting realistic expectations for candidates.

• Developing a recruitment strategy: By working closely with HR and hiring teams, a Talent Acquisition Specialist can develop an effective recruitment strategy. This strategy may include sourcing candidates from various channels, such as job boards, social media platforms, and professional networks.

• Screening and interviewing candidates: Collaboration with HR and hiring teams is essential in the screening and interviewing process. HR teams may handle initial screenings, while hiring teams can conduct technical interviews to assess candidates' skills and fit for the role.

• Providing feedback and recommendations: Throughout the hiring process, a Talent Acquisition Specialist collaborates with HR and hiring teams by providing feedback and recommendations on candidates. This feedback helps in making informed decisions and narrowing down the candidate pool.

• Coordinating the offer and onboarding process: Once a candidate is selected, collaboration with HR and hiring teams continues in coordinating the offer and onboarding process. This involves negotiating the offer, preparing necessary documentation, and ensuring a smooth transition for the new hire.

Real-world example: In a top-tier IT company, the Talent Acquisition Specialist collaborates with HR and hiring teams to fill a Senior Software Engineer position. The collaboration involves understanding the technical requirements, sourcing candidates from relevant platforms, conducting technical interviews with the hiring team, providing feedback on candidates' technical skills, and coordinating the offer and onboarding process.

How do you collaborate with other HR functions, such as compensation & benefits?

Answer

As a Talent Acquisition Specialist specializing in top-tier IT companies, collaboration with other HR functions such as compensation and benefits is crucial to ensure a seamless and effective hiring process.

Here are some ways I collaborate with other HR functions:

1. Regular communication: I maintain open lines of communication with the compensation and benefits team to stay updated on any changes or updates that may impact the hiring process. This helps me align the recruitment strategy with the compensation and benefits structure.

2. Job analysis: I work closely with the compensation and benefits team to conduct a comprehensive job analysis. This involves understanding the skill requirements, market value, and compensation benchmarks for the positions we are hiring for. By collaborating on this analysis, we ensure that the compensation and benefits offered are competitive and attractive to top-tier IT candidates.

3. Salary negotiation: When it comes to salary negotiation with potential candidates, I collaborate with the compensation and benefits team to ensure that we offer a fair and competitive salary package. I rely on their expertise to provide insights on market trends, salary ranges, and any specific compensation policies that need to be considered.

4. Benefits package: I also collaborate with the compensation and benefits team to design and communicate the benefits package for new hires. This includes discussing health insurance, retirement plans, stock options, and other perks that may be offered by the company. By collaborating on the benefits package, we ensure that it aligns with the overall compensation strategy and attracts top talent.

5. Continuous improvement: Collaboration with the compensation and benefits team is not limited to the hiring process. We also work together to analyze and evaluate the effectiveness of our recruitment strategy. This includes reviewing the retention rates, employee satisfaction, and overall cost-effectiveness of the compensation and benefits offered. By collaborating on these aspects, we can identify areas for improvement and make necessary adjustments to enhance the talent acquisition process.

By collaborating with other HR functions, such as compensation and benefits, I ensure that the hiring process is streamlined, competitive, and aligned with the overall HR strategy of the organization.

Discuss your experience with cross-functional collaboration in the hiring process?

Answer

During my tenure as a Talent Acquisition Specialist specializing in top-tier IT companies, I have gained extensive experience with cross-functional collaboration in the hiring process.

Here are some key points:
• Collaborating with various departments such as HR, hiring managers, and team leads to understand the specific job requirements and desired candidate profiles.
• Engaging in regular meetings with stakeholders to align on the hiring strategy, discuss candidate pipelines, and address any concerns or challenges.
• Working closely with the HR team to ensure compliance with company policies and procedures throughout the hiring process.
• Partnering with hiring managers to develop job descriptions that accurately reflect the role's responsibilities and required skills.
• Collaborating with the marketing team to create compelling job advertisements and employer branding materials to attract top talent.
• Collaborating with the technical team to facilitate technical assessments and interviews, ensuring candidates are evaluated effectively.

• Coordinating with the finance team to manage budget allocation for recruitment activities, such as job postings, candidate assessments, and recruitment events.
• Regularly communicating with candidates throughout the hiring process, providing updates, and addressing any questions or concerns.
• Collaborating with the onboarding team to ensure a smooth transition for new hires, sharing relevant candidate information, and facilitating the necessary paperwork.

Overall, my experience with cross-functional collaboration in the hiring process has allowed me to effectively navigate the complexities of talent acquisition, ensuring a seamless and efficient recruitment process for top-tier IT companies.

What strategies do you use to ensure smooth communication with hiring teams?

Answer
1. Establish clear communication channels: I ensure that there are clear communication channels in place to facilitate smooth and effective communication with hiring teams. This includes using tools like email, instant messaging platforms, and project management software to stay in touch and share information.
2. Regular check-ins and updates: I schedule regular check-ins with the hiring teams to provide updates on the status of the recruitment process. This helps in keeping everyone informed and ensures that any issues or concerns are addressed in a timely manner.
3. Active listening: I practice active listening when communicating with hiring teams. This means paying full attention to what the team members are saying, asking clarifying questions, and summarizing key points to ensure that there is a clear understanding of expectations and requirements.
4. Providing timely feedback: I believe in providing timely feedback to the hiring teams. This includes sharing feedback on candidates, interview processes, and any other relevant information. Timely feedback helps in maintaining a smooth flow of communication and ensures that everyone is on the same page.

5. Documentation: I maintain clear and concise documentation of all communication with hiring teams. This includes keeping track of emails, meeting minutes, and any other relevant documentation. Having a record of communication helps in avoiding miscommunication and provides a reference point for future discussions.

How do you align recruitment efforts with broader HR initiatives?

Answer

Understand the broader HR initiatives and goals: As a Talent Acquisition Specialist, it is crucial to have a clear understanding of the broader HR initiatives and goals within the organization. This includes understanding the overall talent acquisition strategy, the company's mission and values, and the specific HR objectives for the year.

Collaborate with HR team: To align recruitment efforts with broader HR initiatives, it is important to collaborate closely with the HR team. This can involve regular meetings and communication to ensure that recruitment efforts are in line with the overall HR strategy. For example, if the HR team has identified diversity and inclusion as a key initiative, the recruitment efforts can focus on sourcing and attracting diverse candidates.

Use data and analytics: Data and analytics play a crucial role in aligning recruitment efforts with broader HR initiatives. By analyzing recruitment metrics such as time to fill, source of hire, and candidate quality, Talent Acquisition Specialists can identify areas for improvement and make data-driven decisions. For example, if the HR initiative is to improve the quality of hires, data analysis can help identify the most effective sourcing channels and screening methods.

Implement employer branding: Employer branding is another important aspect of aligning recruitment efforts with broader HR initiatives. By showcasing the company's culture, values, and employee benefits, Talent Acquisition Specialists can attract candidates who align with the organization's mission. For example, if the HR initiative is to enhance the employer brand as an innovative and tech-driven company, the recruitment efforts can focus on highlighting the company's cutting-edge projects and technology stack.

Provide training and development opportunities: Talent Acquisition Specialists can align recruitment efforts with broader HR initiatives by focusing on candidates' long-term growth and development. This can involve incorporating questions about career goals and aspirations during interviews and promoting learning and development opportunities within the organization. For example, if the HR initiative is to enhance employee engagement and retention, the recruitment efforts can focus on attracting candidates who value continuous learning and career progression.

Regularly evaluate and adapt recruitment strategies: To ensure alignment with broader HR initiatives, it is important to regularly evaluate and adapt recruitment strategies. This can involve gathering feedback from hiring managers, candidates, and HR stakeholders to identify areas for improvement. For example, if the HR initiative is to streamline the recruitment process and reduce time to fill, the recruitment efforts can focus on implementing technology solutions and process improvements.

Summary: Aligning recruitment efforts with broader HR initiatives requires a clear understanding of the HR goals, collaboration with the HR team, use of data and analytics, implementation of employer branding, focus on training and development, and regular evaluation and adaptation of recruitment strategies.

Adaptability and Resilience

Adaptability and resilience are crucial qualities for a Talent Acquisition Specialist, especially when specializing in top-tier IT companies. Adaptability refers to the ability to adjust to new and changing situations, while resilience refers to the ability to bounce back from setbacks and challenges.

Here are some key points to consider regarding adaptability and resilience in the context of a Talent Acquisition Specialist at a top-tier IT company:

• Technology is constantly evolving in the IT industry, and as a Talent Acquisition Specialist, it is important to stay up-to-date with the latest trends and changes in the field. This requires being adaptable and open to learning new technologies and methodologies.
• When hiring for top-tier IT companies, the competition for talent is fierce. There may be instances where a candidate you were targeting for a position is no longer available or has accepted an offer from another company. In such situations, resilience is essential to bounce back quickly and find alternative candidates who meet the requirements of the role.
• Building strong relationships with hiring managers, understanding their needs, and aligning recruitment strategies accordingly is crucial. However, sometimes hiring needs may change unexpectedly due to shifting business priorities or budget constraints. Being adaptable allows the Talent Acquisition Specialist to quickly adjust their strategies and priorities to meet the changing needs of the organization.
• A Talent Acquisition Specialist may also face rejection from candidates during the recruitment process. Resilience is needed to handle rejection and not let it affect the ability to continue sourcing and attracting top talent.

Real-world examples that demonstrate adaptability and resilience in a Talent Acquisition Specialist specializing in top-tier IT companies include:

• Successfully adapting to a sudden change in hiring requirements by quickly pivoting recruitment strategies and focusing on different sourcing channels.

• Overcoming a setback in the hiring process, such as a candidate declining an offer, by promptly identifying alternative candidates and ensuring a smooth transition to the next stage of the recruitment process.

• Adapting to new technologies and tools used in the IT industry to streamline the recruitment process and improve sourcing and candidate assessment.

In summary, adaptability and resilience are essential qualities for a Talent Acquisition Specialist specializing in top-tier IT companies. Being adaptable allows them to adjust to changing circumstances, while resilience helps them bounce back from setbacks and continue sourcing top talent. Real-world examples demonstrate how these qualities can be applied in practice.

How do you adapt your recruitment strategies to changes in the job market?

Answer

- Stay updated on current trends and changes in the job market by attending industry conferences, webinars, and networking events.
- Regularly review and revise job descriptions to align with the evolving needs and requirements of the job market.
- Utilize social media platforms, online job boards, and professional networking sites to reach a wider pool of candidates.
- Leverage data analytics and applicant tracking systems to identify patterns and trends in candidate preferences and behavior.
- Collaborate with hiring managers and department heads to understand their changing staffing needs and tailor recruitment strategies accordingly.
- Develop relationships with universities, coding bootcamps, and other educational institutions to tap into emerging talent pools.

- Offer competitive compensation packages, flexible work arrangements, and other attractive benefits to attract top talent in a competitive job market.
- Provide ongoing training and professional development opportunities to ensure the skills of existing employees remain relevant and up-to-date.
- Regularly evaluate the effectiveness of recruitment strategies through metrics such as time-to-fill, quality-of-hire, and retention rates, and make necessary adjustments.
- Stay proactive and anticipate future changes in the job market, such as emerging technologies or shifts in industry demands, to stay ahead of the competition.

Discuss a situation where you had to pivot your recruitment approach quickly?

Answer

In my role as a Talent Acquisition Specialist specializing in top-tier IT companies, I have encountered situations where I had to quickly pivot my recruitment approach to ensure successful hiring outcomes.

One such situation I can discuss is as follows:

Scenario: The company I was working for had an urgent need to hire a highly skilled software engineer to meet a critical project deadline. However, the traditional recruitment approach of posting job ads and waiting for applications was not generating the desired candidate pool. In order to quickly pivot my recruitment approach, I took the following steps:

1. Re-evaluated the job requirements: I collaborated with the hiring manager and project team to identify the key skills and qualifications needed for the role. This helped me better understand the specific criteria we were looking for in a candidate, enabling me to target my search more effectively.

2. Leveraged my network: I reached out to my network of IT professionals and industry contacts to spread the word about the job opening. This allowed me to tap into a pool of potential candidates who might not be actively looking for new opportunities but could be interested in the role.

3. Utilized social media platforms: I utilized social media platforms, such as LinkedIn and Twitter, to promote the job opening and engage with potential candidates. This helped generate more visibility and attract qualified candidates who might not have come across the traditional job ads.

4. Conducted targeted outreach: I proactively reached out to individuals who had relevant profiles on professional networking sites and attended industry events. By personalizing my outreach and showcasing the exciting aspects of the role and the company, I was able to capture the attention of potential candidates and encourage them to consider the opportunity.

5. Explored alternative sourcing channels: I researched and utilized alternative sourcing channels, such as niche job boards and online communities relevant to the specific technology stack required for the role. This allowed me to tap into specialized talent pools and identify candidates with the desired skills and experience.

Result: By quickly pivoting my recruitment approach and implementing these strategies, I was able to attract a strong pool of qualified candidates within a short period of time. This enabled the hiring team to conduct efficient interviews and make a successful hire, meeting the critical project deadline.

Overall, this experience taught me the importance of agility and adaptability in the recruitment process. It highlighted the need to constantly assess and adjust the approach to ensure the best possible outcome for the organization.

How do you handle rejection or unsuccessful placements in recruitment?

Answer
Recognize that rejection is a normal part of the recruitment process and not a reflection of personal failure.

- Maintain a positive attitude and resilience in the face of rejection.
- Reflect on the reasons for the rejection and learn from the experience.

- Seek feedback from both the candidate and the hiring manager to understand any areas for improvement.
- Take the opportunity to refine and improve recruitment strategies and processes.
- Develop a support network of colleagues and mentors who can provide guidance and encouragement.
- Focus on the successful placements and positive outcomes to maintain motivation.
- Utilize data and analytics to identify patterns and trends that can inform future decision-making.
- Continuously update knowledge and skills in the recruitment field to stay current and competitive.

How do you stay motivated during challenging recruitment periods?

Answer
- Set clear goals and objectives for each recruitment period
- Break down the recruitment process into smaller tasks and focus on completing them one at a time
- Celebrate small wins and achievements to stay motivated
- Seek support and advice from colleagues or mentors
- Stay updated with industry trends and developments to maintain enthusiasm
- Take breaks and engage in activities that help relieve stress and rejuvenate
- Visualize the end result and the positive impact of successful recruitment
- Remind yourself of the value and importance of finding the right talent for the company
- Use positive affirmations and self-motivating techniques to stay focused and energized
- Stay organized and maintain a well-structured recruitment process to avoid feeling overwhelmed

Employment Brand and Employee Referrals

Answer

An employment brand refers to the reputation and image that a company has as an employer. It is the perception of the company as a great place to work and the values, culture, and benefits it offers to its employees.

Employee referrals are a recruitment strategy where current employees recommend potential candidates for job openings within the company. These referrals can be a valuable source of high-quality candidates who are more likely to be a good fit for the company culture and requirements.

The employment brand and employee referrals are closely connected as a strong employment brand can significantly enhance the effectiveness of employee referrals. When a company has a positive employment brand, employees are more likely to recommend their friends and connections to work at the company.

A strong employment brand can also attract more candidates through employee referrals as potential candidates are more likely to be interested in working for a company with a good reputation as an employer.

Here are some real-world examples to illustrate the importance of employment brand and employee referrals:

1. Company A is known for its positive company culture, competitive benefits, and opportunities for career growth. Employees are proud to work for the company and often refer their friends and connections for job openings. As a result, the company receives a high number of qualified candidates through employee referrals, reducing the time and cost of recruitment.

2. Company B has a poor employment brand due to negative reviews about its work environment and lack of opportunities for advancement. As a result, employees are less likely to refer candidates, and the company struggles to attract high-quality candidates through employee referrals.

To summarize, a strong employment brand can enhance the effectiveness of employee referrals by attracting more candidates and increasing the likelihood of employee recommendations. Employee referrals, in turn, can be a valuable source of high-quality candidates who are a good fit for the company culture and requirements.

How do you leverage employee referrals in the recruitment process?

Answer
Employee referrals can be a valuable source of talent in the recruitment process, especially when it comes to top-tier IT companies.

Here are some ways to leverage employee referrals:
1. Establish a formal employee referral program: Create a structured program that encourages employees to refer candidates for open positions. This can include offering incentives or rewards for successful referrals.
2. Communicate the open positions to employees: Keep employees informed about job openings within the company and encourage them to refer qualified candidates. This can be done through regular email updates, internal newsletters, or even company-wide meetings.
3. Train employees on how to make effective referrals: Provide training or guidelines to employees on how to identify and refer potential candidates. This can include providing information on the skills and qualifications needed for specific roles.
4. Provide a user-friendly referral process: Make it easy for employees to submit referrals by creating a user-friendly online portal or referral form. This can streamline the process and encourage more employees to participate.
5. Recognize and reward employee referrals: Show appreciation for employees who make successful referrals by publicly recognizing them or providing additional incentives. This can help create a culture of referral and encourage more employees to participate.
6. Track and measure the effectiveness of employee referrals: Regularly track and analyze the success rate of employee referrals to assess the effectiveness of the program. This can help identify areas for improvement and make necessary adjustments.

By leveraging employee referrals in the recruitment process, top-tier IT companies can tap into their employees' networks and potentially find highly qualified candidates who may not be actively looking for job opportunities. Employee referrals can also lead to higher retention rates and better cultural fit, as referred candidates are often familiar with the company and its values.

For example, a talent acquisition specialist at a top-tier IT company could implement an employee referral program that offers a cash bonus for successful referrals. They could communicate open positions to employees through regular email updates and provide training on how to make effective referrals. The specialist could also create a user-friendly online referral portal and publicly recognize employees who make successful referrals. By tracking and measuring the effectiveness of employee referrals, the specialist can continuously improve the program and leverage this valuable source of talent.

Discuss your experience with building and promoting the employment brand?

Answer

As a Talent Acquisition Specialist specializing in top-tier IT companies, I have extensive experience in building and promoting the employment brand. Here are some key points to discuss my experience:

Developing an employment brand strategy: I have worked closely with the marketing and HR teams to develop a comprehensive employment brand strategy. This involved identifying the unique selling points of the company, understanding the target audience, and creating compelling messaging to attract top talent.

Creating engaging employer branding materials: I have collaborated with graphic designers and content writers to create visually appealing and informative materials such as career websites, brochures, videos, and social media posts. These materials effectively showcase the company culture, values, and career opportunities to potential candidates.

Leveraging social media and online platforms: I have utilized various social media platforms like LinkedIn, Twitter, and Facebook to promote the employment brand. This includes regularly posting job openings, sharing employee testimonials, and highlighting company achievements. Additionally, I have optimized the company's career website for search engines to increase its visibility and reach.

Participating in industry events and job fairs: I have represented the company at industry events and job fairs to establish a strong presence and engage with potential candidates. This includes setting up attractive booth displays, conducting informative presentations, and networking with industry professionals.

Monitoring and measuring brand effectiveness: I have implemented tracking mechanisms to monitor the effectiveness of the employment brand strategy. This includes analyzing website traffic, social media engagement, and candidate feedback. By regularly reviewing these metrics, I have been able to make data-driven adjustments to optimize the brand promotion efforts.

Real-world example: In my previous role, I successfully built and promoted the employment brand for a top-tier IT company. By implementing a targeted social media campaign and creating engaging employer branding materials, we saw a significant increase in qualified candidate applications. The company's reputation as an employer of choice also improved, leading to higher employee retention rates and a positive impact on overall company culture.

Overall, my experience with building and promoting the employment brand has been focused on creating a strong and appealing image of the company to attract top talent. I have utilized various strategies, tools, and platforms to effectively communicate the company's values, culture, and career opportunities to potential candidates.

What steps do you take to ensure a consistent message in recruitment marketing?

Answer

To ensure a consistent message in recruitment marketing, I take the following steps:

1. Defining the employer brand: I work closely with the HR and marketing teams to clearly define the employer brand. This involves understanding the company's values, culture, and unique selling points to create a compelling message that resonates with top-tier IT professionals.

2. Developing a recruitment marketing strategy: I create a comprehensive recruitment marketing strategy that aligns with the employer brand. This strategy includes identifying target audiences, determining the most effective channels to reach them, and developing key messages that highlight the company's strengths and opportunities for growth.

3. Creating consistent messaging: I ensure that all recruitment marketing materials, including job postings, social media content, and email campaigns, have a consistent message. This means using the same tone, language, and key selling points across different platforms to create a cohesive and recognizable brand presence.

4. Training and educating hiring managers: I work with hiring managers to ensure they understand the employer brand and can effectively communicate it during the recruitment process. This may involve conducting training sessions, providing resources and guidelines, and regularly communicating updates.

5. Monitoring and evaluating results: I regularly monitor the effectiveness of recruitment marketing campaigns to ensure the message is resonating with the target audience. This includes tracking metrics such as the number of qualified applicants, conversion rates, and candidate feedback. Based on the results, I make adjustments and refinements to the messaging as needed.

By following these steps, I can ensure a consistent message in recruitment marketing that attracts top-tier IT professionals and accurately represents the employer brand.

How do you incorporate employee testimonials in recruitment efforts?

Answer

Employee testimonials can be a powerful tool in recruitment efforts as they provide firsthand accounts of the employee experience and can help attract top talent. Here are some ways to incorporate employee testimonials:

1. Create a dedicated testimonial page on the company website: This page can feature written testimonials from current employees, highlighting their positive experiences and why they chose to work for the company. Including photos and job titles can add credibility and help potential candidates relate to the testimonials.

2. Share testimonials on social media platforms: Social media platforms like LinkedIn, Facebook, and Instagram can be used to share employee testimonials. These platforms have a wide reach and can help generate interest in the company.

3. Feature testimonials in job postings: Including snippets or quotes from employee testimonials in job postings can help attract candidates by showcasing the positive aspects of working for the company.

4. Use testimonials in recruitment presentations: When conducting recruitment presentations, incorporating employee testimonials can provide real-world examples of the company culture and employee satisfaction. This can help candidates envision themselves working for the company.

5. Include testimonials in recruitment marketing materials: Employee testimonials can be included in brochures, pamphlets, or other marketing materials that are used to attract potential candidates. This can provide an authentic perspective on what it's like to work for the company.

By incorporating employee testimonials in recruitment efforts, companies can showcase the positive aspects of their culture and attract top talent who resonate with the experiences of current employees.

Time Management and Prioritization

Time management and prioritization are crucial skills for a Talent Acquisition Specialist specializing in top-tier IT companies.

Effective time management allows a Talent Acquisition Specialist to maximize productivity, meet deadlines, and ensure that the recruitment process runs smoothly.

Prioritization is the process of determining which tasks are most important and should be tackled first.

Here are some key strategies for time management and prioritization in talent acquisition:

• Set clear objectives: Clearly define the goals and objectives of each recruitment project. This helps in prioritizing tasks and allocating time accordingly.

• Create a schedule: Develop a detailed schedule or calendar that outlines the tasks and deadlines for each recruitment project. This helps in organizing and prioritizing tasks effectively.

• Use a to-do list: Maintain a to-do list to keep track of all the tasks that need to be completed. Prioritize the tasks based on their importance and urgency.

• Identify and eliminate time-wasters: Identify activities that consume a significant amount of time but do not contribute to the recruitment process. Eliminate or minimize these time-wasters to free up time for more important tasks.

• Delegate tasks: Delegate tasks that can be done by others, such as scheduling interviews or conducting initial screenings. This helps in freeing up time for high-priority tasks.

• Use technology: Utilize technology tools and software to streamline and automate repetitive tasks, such as resume screening or interview scheduling. This saves time and allows for better focus on important tasks.

• Break down complex tasks: If a task seems overwhelming, break it down into smaller, manageable tasks. This makes it easier to prioritize and allocate time for each sub-task.

• Practice effective communication: Efficient communication with hiring managers, candidates, and other stakeholders is essential for effective time management and prioritization.

Real-world example:

Imagine a Talent Acquisition Specialist working for a top-tier IT company that is looking to hire multiple software engineers within a tight deadline. The specialist needs to manage the entire recruitment process, from sourcing candidates to conducting interviews and making job offers.

To manage time effectively, the specialist sets clear objectives for each stage of the recruitment process, such as sourcing, screening, and interviewing. They create a schedule that outlines the tasks and deadlines for each stage. They use a to-do list to prioritize tasks and identify any time-wasting activities that can be eliminated.

The specialist delegates tasks such as resume screening and initial screenings to a recruitment coordinator, freeing up time for high-priority tasks like conducting technical interviews. They also use technology tools like an applicant tracking system and interview scheduling software to automate repetitive tasks and streamline the process.

By practicing effective communication with hiring managers and candidates, the specialist ensures that there are no delays or miscommunications during the recruitment process.

Summary:
Time management and prioritization are crucial skills for a Talent Acquisition Specialist.
Key strategies include setting clear objectives, creating a schedule, using a to-do list, identifying and eliminating time-wasters, delegating tasks, using technology, breaking down complex tasks, and practicing effective communication.

A real-world example demonstrates how these strategies can be applied in the recruitment process for a top-tier IT company.

How do you manage your time effectively when working on multiple recruitment projects?

Answer

1. Prioritize tasks: Identify the most important and urgent tasks and focus on completing them first. This can be done by creating a to-do list or using a project management tool.

2. Set clear goals and deadlines: Clearly define the goals and deadlines for each project. This will help in managing time effectively and staying on track.

3. Break down tasks: Break down larger tasks into smaller, manageable tasks. This will make it easier to allocate time for each task and track progress.

4. Delegate tasks: If possible, delegate some tasks to other team members or external resources. This will help in distributing the workload and freeing up time for other projects.

5. Avoid multitasking: Multitasking can lead to decreased productivity and increased errors. Instead, focus on one task at a time and give it your full attention.

6. Use time management techniques: Utilize time management techniques such as the Pomodoro Technique or time-blocking to improve productivity and manage time effectively.

7. Stay organized: Keep all project-related documents, emails, and communication in one place. This will help in avoiding confusion and saving time searching for information.

8. Communicate and collaborate: Regularly communicate with stakeholders, team members, and candidates to ensure everyone is on the same page. Collaboration can help in streamlining the recruitment process and saving time.

9. Learn from experience: Reflect on past recruitment projects and identify areas for improvement. This will help in refining time management strategies and optimizing future projects.

Discuss a situation where you had to meet tight deadlines in recruitment?

Answer

In my previous role as a Talent Acquisition Specialist specializing in top-tier IT companies, I frequently encountered situations where I had to meet tight deadlines in recruitment. One such situation that comes to mind is when we had to hire a team of software engineers for a high-priority project within a very short timeframe.

I was given a deadline of two weeks to source, screen, and hire five software engineers with specific technical skills. This was particularly challenging because the market for top-tier software engineers was highly competitive, and there was a limited pool of candidates with the required skills.

To meet the tight deadline, I employed several strategies:

1. Active sourcing: I proactively searched for potential candidates on various platforms, including LinkedIn, job boards, and professional networks. This involved reaching out to passive candidates and convincing them to consider the opportunity. I also leveraged my network to get referrals from industry professionals who might know suitable candidates.

2. Streamlined screening process: I developed a streamlined screening process to quickly assess candidates' technical skills and cultural fit. This involved conducting initial phone screens to evaluate their technical abilities and conducting in-depth interviews to assess their cultural fit with the organization.

3. Collaborative decision-making: I worked closely with the hiring managers and project stakeholders to ensure a quick and efficient decision-making process. We held regular meetings to discuss candidate feedback and make timely decisions to move candidates through the hiring process.

4. Negotiation skills: As the deadline loomed closer, I had to negotiate job offers with the selected candidates to ensure they accepted our offer and joined the team within the desired timeframe. This involved understanding their motivations and addressing any concerns they had about the role or the organization.

Despite the tight deadline and challenges, I successfully hired five highly skilled software engineers within the two-week timeframe. This was achieved through a combination of active sourcing, streamlined screening, collaborative decision-making, and effective negotiation skills.

What strategies do you use to prioritize urgent and important recruitment tasks?

Answer

To prioritize urgent and important recruitment tasks, I use the following strategies:

• Assess the urgency and importance of each task: I evaluate each recruitment task based on its urgency and importance. Urgent tasks require immediate attention and cannot be delayed, while important tasks contribute to the long-term success of the recruitment process.

• Use a task matrix: I create a task matrix or a priority matrix to visually categorize tasks based on their urgency and importance. This matrix helps me identify which tasks are both urgent and important, allowing me to prioritize them accordingly.

• Seek input from stakeholders: I involve key stakeholders, such as hiring managers or team leaders, in the prioritization process. Their input helps me understand the impact and urgency of certain tasks from their perspective, enabling me to make informed decisions.

• Focus on critical roles and positions: I prioritize recruitment tasks related to critical roles or positions that are essential for the success of the organization. These positions may have a significant impact on the company's growth or operations, making them a top priority.

• Delegate and collaborate: If there are multiple urgent and important tasks, I delegate some of them to capable team members or collaborate with colleagues to share the workload. This ensures that tasks are completed efficiently and effectively.

• Regularly review and adjust priorities: As the recruitment process evolves, priorities may change. I regularly review and adjust priorities based on new information, feedback, or changes in business needs. This helps me stay adaptable and responsive to emerging priorities.

How do you ensure efficiency in the recruitment process?

Answer

To ensure efficiency in the recruitment process as a Talent Acquisition Specialist specializing in top-tier IT companies, the following strategies can be implemented:

• Utilize technology: Leverage applicant tracking systems (ATS) to streamline and automate the recruitment process. These systems help in managing candidate applications, scheduling interviews, and tracking the progress of each candidate.,

• Clear job descriptions: Create detailed and accurate job descriptions that clearly outline the skills, qualifications, and responsibilities required for the role. This helps attract candidates who are a good fit and reduces the number of unqualified applicants.,

• Effective screening: Develop a standardized screening process that includes phone or video interviews, skills assessments, and behavioral assessments. This helps in efficiently evaluating candidates and identifying the most qualified individuals.,

• Collaboration with hiring managers: Work closely with hiring managers to understand their specific requirements and preferences. This collaboration ensures that only the most suitable candidates are presented to the hiring manager, saving time and effort.,

• Proactive sourcing: Actively search for potential candidates through various channels, including job boards, professional networks, and social media. This proactive approach helps in building a pipeline of qualified candidates, reducing the time to fill open positions.,

• Streamlined interview process: Implement a structured interview process that includes a set of standardized questions for each candidate. This ensures consistency and fairness in the evaluation process and allows for efficient comparison of candidates.,

• Timely communication: Maintain regular and timely communication with candidates throughout the recruitment process. This helps in keeping candidates engaged and informed, reducing the risk of losing top talent due to lack of communication.,

• Continuous improvement: Regularly review and analyze recruitment metrics to identify areas for improvement. This includes analyzing time-to-fill, source of hire, and candidate feedback. By continuously improving the recruitment process, efficiency can be maximized.,

Real-world example: In Google, the talent specialist uses an applicant tracking system to manage the entire recruitment process. The system allows them to automate tasks such as resume screening, interview scheduling, and candidate communication, saving significant time and effort.

Leadership and Mentorship

Leadership and mentorship are crucial skills for a Talent Acquisition Specialist specializing in top-tier IT companies. These skills help in effectively guiding and developing talent in the organization.

Leadership involves providing direction, setting goals, and motivating team members to achieve those goals. A Talent Acquisition Specialist with strong leadership skills can effectively manage recruitment processes, make strategic decisions, and drive the team towards success.

Mentorship, on the other hand, involves providing guidance, support, and knowledge sharing to help individuals grow and develop their careers. A Talent Acquisition Specialist with strong mentorship skills can provide valuable insights, share industry best practices, and help individuals navigate their career paths.

Here are some key aspects of leadership and mentorship for a Talent Acquisition Specialist:

• Setting clear goals and expectations for the recruitment team
• Leading by example and demonstrating the desired behaviors and values
• Providing regular feedback and coaching to team members
• Empowering and motivating team members to take on challenges and grow
• Building strong relationships with hiring managers and stakeholders
• Keeping up-to-date with industry trends and best practices
• Actively seeking opportunities to mentor and develop talent within the organization

A real-world example of leadership and mentorship in talent acquisition could be a Talent Acquisition Specialist leading a team in a top-tier IT company to successfully recruit highly skilled software developers. They set clear goals for the team, provide regular feedback and coaching, and empower team members to make independent decisions. Additionally, they actively mentor and develop junior recruiters, helping them enhance their skills and advance in their careers.

How do you lead and mentor junior members of the recruitment team?

Answer

Set clear expectations and goals for junior members of the team, ensuring they understand their role and responsibilities.

Provide ongoing guidance and support to junior team members, offering feedback and constructive criticism to help them improve.

Offer training and development opportunities to enhance their skills and knowledge.

Encourage collaboration and teamwork among team members, fostering a supportive and inclusive environment.

Lead by example, demonstrating professionalism, integrity, and a strong work ethic.

Delegate tasks and responsibilities to junior team members, allowing them to take ownership and learn from their experiences.

Provide regular performance evaluations and coaching sessions to address any areas for improvement and recognize achievements.

Create a culture of continuous learning and growth, encouraging junior team members to seek out new challenges and expand their expertise.

Act as a mentor and role model, sharing insights and lessons learned from personal experiences in the field.

Promote a positive and motivating work environment, celebrating successes and fostering a sense of camaraderie.

Offer opportunities for career advancement and progression within the recruitment team, setting clear pathways for growth and development.

Provide resources and tools to support junior team members in their day-to-day tasks, such as technology platforms and templates for efficient workflow.

An example of when you provided guidance to a less experienced team member?

Answer

Yes, I can share an example of when I provided guidance to a less experienced team member.

In my previous role as a Talent Acquisition Specialist at a top-tier IT company, I had the opportunity to mentor a junior recruiter who was new to the industry and had limited experience.

One specific example that comes to mind is when the junior recruiter was struggling with sourcing candidates for a highly technical role.

I took the time to sit down with them and explain the different strategies and tools that could be used to find qualified candidates in the IT field.

I provided them with a step-by-step guide on how to search for candidates on various job boards, professional networking sites, and social media platforms.

I also shared some best practices for writing compelling job descriptions and reaching out to potential candidates.

To further support their learning, I created a visual aid in the form of a flowchart that outlined the entire candidate sourcing process.

This flowchart included details on each step, such as identifying keywords, filtering search results, and engaging with candidates.

I explained each component of the flowchart in detail and encouraged the junior recruiter to refer to it whenever they needed guidance.

Additionally, I assigned them a hands-on exercise where they had to source candidates for a specific role and present their findings to the team.

I provided feedback on their approach and suggestions for improvement, which helped them gain confidence and refine their skills.

Over time, the junior recruiter became more proficient in candidate sourcing and was able to independently handle similar tasks.

By providing guidance, real-world examples, visual aids, hands-on exercises, and ongoing feedback, I was able to support the development and growth of the less experienced team member.

What leadership qualities do you believe are crucial for success in recruitment?

Answer

1. Strong communication skills: Effective communication is essential for a talent acquisition specialist as they need to clearly convey job requirements, expectations, and company culture to potential candidates. They should be able to articulate the value proposition of the organization and engage candidates in meaningful conversations. 2. Relationship building: Building strong relationships with hiring managers, candidates, and other stakeholders is crucial for success in recruitment. A talent acquisition specialist should be able to establish trust, credibility, and rapport with both internal and external parties. This can be done through active listening, empathy, and understanding of their needs. 3. Strategic thinking: Recruitment is not just about filling positions; it requires a strategic approach to attract and retain top talent. A successful talent acquisition specialist should have the ability to think critically, analyze market trends, and develop innovative sourcing strategies to stay ahead of the competition. 4. Adaptability and flexibility: The recruitment landscape is constantly changing, and a talent acquisition specialist needs to be adaptable and flexible in their approach. They should be able to quickly adjust their sourcing strategies, recruitment processes, and candidate evaluation methods to meet the evolving needs of the organization. 5. Leadership and influence: A talent acquisition specialist should possess strong leadership skills to drive the recruitment process effectively. They should be able to inspire and motivate the team, lead by example, and influence stakeholders to make informed hiring decisions. 6. Problem-solving skills: Recruitment involves dealing with challenges and obstacles throughout the process. A successful talent acquisition specialist should have strong problem-solving skills to overcome any hurdles that may arise. They should be able to think creatively, find alternative solutions, and make data-driven decisions. 7. Continuous learning mindset: The recruitment landscape is dynamic, and it is essential for a talent acquisition specialist to have a continuous learning mindset. They

should stay updated with the latest industry trends, technologies, and best practices to enhance their recruitment strategies and improve their overall performance. 8. Resilience: Recruitment can be a demanding and high-pressure job. A talent acquisition specialist should have resilience and the ability to bounce back from setbacks. They should have the determination to keep going, even in the face of challenges or rejection. 9. Time management: Effective time management is crucial for success in recruitment. A talent acquisition specialist should be able to prioritize tasks, meet deadlines, and handle multiple recruitment processes simultaneously. 10. Emotional intelligence: Recruitment involves dealing with people from diverse backgrounds and personalities. A talent acquisition specialist should have emotional intelligence to understand and manage the emotions of candidates, hiring managers, and other stakeholders. They should be able to navigate difficult conversations, handle conflicts, and build positive relationships.

How do you foster a positive and collaborative team culture?

Answer
1. Lead by example: As a Talent Acquisition Specialist, it is important to lead by example and exhibit positive and collaborative behavior. This includes being respectful, inclusive, and supportive of team members. By demonstrating these qualities, you set the tone for the team and encourage others to do the same.
2. Encourage open communication: Foster a culture of open communication where team members feel comfortable sharing their ideas, concerns, and feedback. This can be done through regular team meetings, one-on-one check-ins, and creating opportunities for collaboration and brainstorming sessions. By encouraging open communication, you create a space for collaboration and ensure that everyone's voice is heard and valued.
3. Establish shared goals and values: Set clear and shared goals for the team and ensure that everyone understands and aligns with the values of the organization. This helps create a sense of purpose and unity within the team. When team members have a common goal

and shared values, they are more likely to work collaboratively and support each other.

4. Recognize and celebrate achievements: Acknowledge and celebrate the achievements and contributions of team members. This can be done through public recognition, rewards, or team-building activities. By recognizing and celebrating achievements, you create a positive and motivating environment that encourages collaboration and teamwork.

5. Foster a culture of learning and development: Encourage continuous learning and development within the team. Provide opportunities for skill enhancement, training programs, and knowledge sharing sessions. By fostering a culture of learning and development, you not only help team members grow professionally but also promote collaboration as they share their learnings and expertise with each other.

Global Talent Acquisition

Global talent acquisition refers to the process of recruiting and hiring top talent from around the world to meet the workforce needs of a global organization.

In today's interconnected world, companies are increasingly looking beyond their local talent pool to find the best candidates for their open positions. This is especially true for top-tier IT companies that require highly skilled professionals in various technology fields.

Global talent acquisition involves sourcing, attracting, and assessing candidates from different countries and cultural backgrounds. It requires a strategic approach to identify and engage with potential candidates who possess the desired skills and experiences.

To effectively carry out global talent acquisition, talent acquisition specialists specializing in top-tier IT companies employ various strategies and techniques. These include:

• Building a strong employer brand: Top-tier IT companies need to establish a strong employer brand that appeals to candidates worldwide. This involves showcasing the company's culture, values, and opportunities for career growth.

• Utilizing multiple recruitment channels: Talent acquisition specialists use various recruitment channels, such as online job boards, social media platforms, and professional networking sites, to reach a global audience. They also partner with recruitment agencies in different countries to tap into their networks.

• Conducting targeted talent searches: Talent acquisition specialists proactively search for top talent in specific technology fields by leveraging online platforms, attending industry events, and engaging with relevant communities and forums. This allows them to identify and connect with candidates who may not be actively looking for new opportunities.

• Assessing candidates' cultural fit: In addition to evaluating candidates' technical skills and qualifications, talent acquisition specialists also assess their cultural fit within the organization. This involves considering factors such as language proficiency, adaptability to different work environments, and ability to collaborate with diverse teams.

Real-world example:

For example, a top-tier IT company based in the United States may be looking to expand its operations in Europe. The company's talent acquisition specialist will need to identify and attract candidates with the necessary skills and language proficiency to work in the European market. They may partner with local recruitment agencies, attend technology conferences in Europe, and leverage online platforms to source and engage with potential candidates.

Summarizing the answer:

Global talent acquisition is the process of recruiting and hiring top talent from around the world to meet the workforce needs of global organizations. Talent acquisition specialists specializing in top-tier IT companies employ various strategies, such as building a strong employer brand, utilizing multiple recruitment channels, conducting targeted talent searches, and assessing candidates' cultural fit. Real-world examples include expanding operations into new markets and partnering with local agencies to source candidates.

How do you approach recruitment for international roles and diverse cultural backgrounds?

Answer

Research and understand the cultural nuances and specific requirements of the target country or region.

Develop a diverse sourcing strategy to attract candidates from different cultural backgrounds.

Collaborate with local recruiters or experts in the target country or region to gain insights and leverage their networks.

Create job postings and marketing materials that showcase the company's commitment to diversity and inclusivity.

Conduct effective interviews that assess both technical skills and cultural fit.

Provide clear and transparent communication throughout the recruitment process, addressing any concerns or questions candidates may have.

Educate hiring managers and key stakeholders on the importance of diversity and how it contributes to the success of the organization.

Offer cultural orientation and onboarding programs to help new hires navigate the company culture and work environment.

Regularly evaluate and review recruitment strategies to ensure they are inclusive and effective in attracting diverse talent.

Discuss your experience with global talent acquisition strategies?

Answer

In my role as a Talent Acquisition Specialist specializing in top-tier IT companies, I have extensive experience in implementing and executing global talent acquisition strategies. Some key points about my experience include:

Developing a comprehensive global talent acquisition strategy that aligns with the company's business goals and objectives.

Utilizing a mix of recruitment channels and techniques to attract top talent from around the world, including online job boards, social media platforms, professional networking sites, and industry events.

Building and maintaining a strong employer brand to attract candidates from different countries and cultures. This includes showcasing the company's values, benefits, and opportunities for growth.

Leveraging technology and data analytics to track and measure the effectiveness of talent acquisition strategies, including candidate sourcing, selection, and onboarding processes.

Working closely with hiring managers and HR teams in different countries to ensure a seamless and efficient recruitment process, while also considering local laws and regulations.

Developing and implementing diversity and inclusion initiatives to attract and retain a diverse pool of candidates from different backgrounds and experiences.

Staying up-to-date with the latest trends and best practices in global talent acquisition, attending conferences, webinars, and networking events to expand my knowledge and skills.

Real-world examples of my experience with global talent acquisition strategies include successfully sourcing and hiring candidates from various countries to fill specialized IT roles, such as software developers, data scientists, and cybersecurity experts.

In summary, my experience with global talent acquisition strategies includes developing comprehensive strategies, utilizing various recruitment channels, building a strong employer brand, leveraging technology and data analytics, collaborating with international teams, promoting diversity and inclusion, and staying updated with industry trends.

What challenges do you anticipate in international recruitment, and how do you overcome them?

Answer

Language and cultural barriers: International recruitment often involves dealing with candidates who speak different languages and come from different cultural backgrounds. This can create challenges in communication and understanding. To overcome these challenges, we can:

• Use language proficiency tests to ensure candidates have the necessary language skills for the job.

• Provide cultural sensitivity training to recruiters to help them understand and appreciate different cultural norms and practices.

• Use video interviews to assess candidates' communication skills and cultural fit.

Legal and regulatory compliance: Different countries have different laws and regulations related to employment and immigration. It can be challenging to navigate these legal requirements and ensure compliance. To overcome these challenges, we can:

• Partner with legal experts who specialize in international employment law to ensure we are following all necessary regulations.

• Stay updated on changes in immigration policies and work permit requirements in different countries.

• Establish clear processes and documentation for visa sponsorship and work permit applications.

Time zones and logistics: International recruitment often involves coordinating interviews, meetings, and other interactions across

different time zones. This can create scheduling challenges and logistical issues. To overcome these challenges, we can:
• Use scheduling tools that can automatically convert time zones and suggest suitable meeting times.
• Be flexible with interview and meeting times to accommodate candidates from different time zones.
• Leverage technology to conduct virtual interviews and assessments, reducing the need for travel and physical logistics.

Summary:
International recruitment comes with its own set of challenges, including language and cultural barriers, legal and regulatory compliance, and time zones and logistics. By implementing strategies such as language proficiency tests, cultural sensitivity training, partnering with legal experts, staying updated on immigration policies, using scheduling tools, and leveraging technology, we can overcome these challenges and successfully recruit top talent from around the world.

How do you ensure consistency in recruitment practices across different regions?

Answer
Establish clear and standardized recruitment processes: Create a set of standardized recruitment procedures and guidelines that clearly outline the steps to be followed in the recruitment process. This will ensure consistency in the way candidates are sourced, screened, interviewed, and evaluated across different regions.
Provide comprehensive training: Conduct regular training sessions for recruiters in different regions to ensure they are well-versed with the standardized recruitment processes. This will help them understand the importance of consistency and enable them to execute the recruitment practices effectively.
Use a centralized applicant tracking system (ATS): Implement an ATS that can be accessed by recruiters in all regions. This will enable them to track candidates, share feedback, and maintain a centralized database of applicants. A centralized ATS ensures that all

recruiters follow the same process and have access to the same information, leading to consistency in recruitment practices.

Establish communication channels: Set up regular meetings or virtual conferences to facilitate communication and knowledge sharing among recruiters in different regions. This will help in clarifying doubts, discussing best practices, and ensuring alignment in recruitment practices across regions.

Monitor and evaluate recruitment metrics: Establish key performance indicators (KPIs) for recruitment and regularly monitor and evaluate them across different regions. This will help identify any variations or deviations from the standardized processes and take corrective actions to ensure consistency.

Conduct regular audits: Periodically conduct audits of recruitment processes in different regions to ensure compliance with the standardized procedures. These audits can help identify any gaps or inconsistencies and provide an opportunity for process improvement.

Real-world example: A top-tier IT company has recruitment teams in different regions across the globe. To ensure consistency in recruitment practices, the company has established a comprehensive recruitment handbook that provides detailed guidelines for each stage of the recruitment process. Recruiters undergo regular training sessions to understand and implement these guidelines. The company also uses a centralized ATS that enables recruiters to track candidates, share feedback, and maintain a centralized database of applicants. Regular communication channels and virtual conferences are set up to facilitate knowledge sharing and alignment. Recruitment metrics are monitored and evaluated, and periodic audits are conducted to ensure compliance and identify areas for improvement.

Metrics and Reporting

Metrics and reporting are crucial aspects of talent acquisition as they provide valuable insights into the effectiveness of the recruitment process and help in making data-driven decisions.

Here are some key metrics and reporting practices for a Talent Acquisition Specialist specializing in top-tier IT companies:

• Time to fill: This metric measures the time taken to fill a job vacancy from the moment it is opened. It helps assess the efficiency of the recruitment process and identify any bottlenecks or delays. For example, a longer time to fill may indicate that the sourcing strategy needs improvement or that the job requirements are unrealistic.

• Quality of hire: This metric evaluates the performance and retention of new hires. It can be measured based on their job performance, feedback from managers, and their tenure with the company. A high-quality hire is someone who meets or exceeds the expectations of the role and stays with the company for a significant period.

• Source of hire: This metric tracks the channels or sources through which candidates are recruited. It helps determine the most effective sourcing strategies and allocate resources accordingly. For example, if a large number of quality hires are coming from employee referrals, it indicates the need to invest more in employee referral programs.

• Cost per hire: This metric calculates the total cost incurred in hiring a new employee. It includes expenses for job advertisements, recruitment agency fees, background checks, and onboarding. Monitoring the cost per hire helps in optimizing the recruitment budget and identifying cost-saving opportunities.

• Applicant tracking system (ATS) utilization: An ATS is a software that streamlines the recruitment process by automating tasks like resume screening and interview scheduling. Tracking the utilization of the ATS provides insights into its effectiveness and helps identify areas for improvement. For example, if the ATS is underutilized, it may indicate a lack of training or awareness among recruiters.

In terms of reporting, Talent Acquisition Specialists should provide regular updates to stakeholders, such as hiring managers and HR leaders, on the recruitment metrics and their implications. Reports should be tailored to the audience and highlight key findings, trends, and actionable insights.

To summarize, metrics and reporting are essential for a Talent Acquisition Specialist specializing in top-tier IT companies. They help in assessing the efficiency of the recruitment process, evaluating the quality of hires, optimizing sourcing strategies, managing recruitment costs, and improving the utilization of recruitment technology.

What recruitment metrics do you track, and how do you use them to inform decision-making?

Answer

As a Talent Acquisition Specialist specializing in top-tier IT companies, I track several key recruitment metrics to inform decision-making. These metrics help me assess the effectiveness of my recruitment strategies and make data-driven decisions. Some of the recruitment metrics I track include:

• Time to fill: This metric measures the number of days it takes to fill a vacant position. By tracking time to fill, I can identify any bottlenecks in the recruitment process and take steps to streamline it. For example, if the time to fill is consistently high for a particular role, it may indicate that the job description or sourcing channels need to be revised to attract more qualified candidates.

• Cost per hire: This metric calculates the average cost incurred to hire a new employee. It includes expenses such as advertising, recruitment agency fees, and onboarding costs. By tracking cost per hire, I can evaluate the efficiency of different recruitment channels and make informed decisions about where to allocate resources.

• Candidate quality: This metric assesses the quality of candidates who progress through the recruitment process. It can be measured through various indicators, such as the percentage of candidates who reach the final interview stage or the percentage of candidates who accept job offers. By tracking candidate quality, I can identify areas for improvement in the screening and selection process and make adjustments accordingly.

• Source of hire: This metric tracks the sources from which successful hires originate. It provides insights into the most effective recruitment channels and helps me allocate resources to those channels that yield the best results. For example, if a significant number of successful hires are coming from employee referrals, I may consider implementing an employee referral program to further leverage this source of talent.

• Diversity metrics: In addition to the above metrics, I also track diversity metrics to ensure a diverse and inclusive hiring process. These metrics include the percentage of diverse candidates in the applicant pool, the representation of different demographic groups at each stage of the recruitment process, and the diversity of the final hires. By tracking diversity metrics, I can identify any biases or barriers in the recruitment process and implement strategies to promote diversity and inclusion.

Discuss your experience with creating and presenting recruitment reports?

Answer

I have extensive experience in creating and presenting recruitment reports as a Talent Acquisition Specialist specializing in top-tier IT companies.

I have developed a systematic approach to creating recruitment reports that includes the following steps:

• Gathering data: I collect relevant data such as the number of open positions, the number of applicants, the source of applicants, and the time-to-fill for each position.

• Analyzing data: I analyze the data to identify trends and patterns in the recruitment process. For example, I look for any bottlenecks or areas of improvement.

• Creating visual reports: I use tools like Excel or data visualization software to create visual reports that are easy to understand and visually appealing. These reports include charts, graphs, and tables to present the data in a clear and concise manner.

• Presenting reports: I present the reports to key stakeholders, such as hiring managers or senior leadership. I explain the findings and provide recommendations for improving the recruitment process if necessary.

Real-world examples of my experience with creating and presenting recruitment reports include:
• I created a recruitment report for an IT company that showed a high number of applicants from a specific job board. Based on this data, we decided to invest more in advertising on that job board to attract top talent.
• I presented a recruitment report to senior leadership that highlighted a long time-to-fill for certain positions. As a result, we implemented a streamlined interview process and reduced the time-to-fill by 30%.

To summarize, I have a strong track record of creating and presenting recruitment reports that provide valuable insights and drive improvements in the recruitment process. I use a systematic approach, utilize visual aids, and present the findings to key stakeholders.

How do you measure the success of your recruitment efforts?

Answer
To measure the success of recruitment efforts for a Talent Acquisition Specialist specializing in top-tier IT companies, the following metrics and methods can be used:
• Time to fill: This measures the average number of days it takes to fill a job opening. A shorter time to fill indicates a more efficient recruitment process.
• Quality of hire: This metric assesses the performance and impact of new hires. It can be measured through performance reviews, manager feedback, and retention rates.
• Cost per hire: This measures the total cost incurred to fill a job opening. It includes advertising costs, recruiter fees, and other recruitment expenses. A lower cost per hire indicates cost-effective recruitment strategies.

• Candidate satisfaction: This metric gauges the satisfaction level of candidates throughout the recruitment process. It can be measured through surveys or feedback forms.

• Diversity and inclusion: This metric evaluates the diversity and inclusion efforts in the recruitment process. It measures the percentage of diverse candidates hired and the effectiveness of diversity initiatives.

Real-world examples of how these metrics can be applied to measure recruitment success in top-tier IT companies include:

• Time to fill: If the average time to fill IT positions is significantly shorter compared to industry benchmarks, it indicates the effectiveness of the recruitment process in attracting and selecting qualified candidates quickly.

• Quality of hire: Assessing the performance of new hires by comparing their productivity, technical skills, and contribution to projects against established benchmarks can determine the success of recruitment efforts.

• Cost per hire: Tracking the cost per hire for IT positions and benchmarking it against industry averages can help identify cost-saving opportunities and optimize recruitment strategies.

• Candidate satisfaction: Conducting post-recruitment surveys or feedback sessions with candidates to assess their overall experience and satisfaction levels can provide insights into the effectiveness of the recruitment process.

• Diversity and inclusion: Monitoring the diversity metrics of hired candidates, such as gender, ethnicity, and background, and comparing them to diversity targets and industry benchmarks can measure the success of diversity and inclusion initiatives.

In summary, the success of recruitment efforts can be measured through metrics such as time to fill, quality of hire, cost per hire, candidate satisfaction, and diversity and inclusion. These metrics provide objective data to evaluate and improve the effectiveness of the recruitment process in top-tier IT companies.

What steps do you take to address areas for improvement based on metrics?

Answer

Analyze the metrics: The first step is to analyze the metrics to identify areas that need improvement. This can be done by studying the data and identifying patterns or trends that indicate areas of weakness or inefficiency.

Set clear objectives: Once the areas for improvement have been identified, it is important to set clear objectives for addressing these areas. This involves defining specific and measurable goals that can be used to track progress.

Develop an action plan: With clear objectives in place, the next step is to develop an action plan for addressing the areas of improvement. This plan should outline the specific steps that need to be taken, as well as the resources and timeline required.

Implement changes: Once the action plan has been developed, it is important to implement the necessary changes to address the areas of improvement. This may involve making changes to processes, procedures, or systems, as well as providing training or support to employees.

Monitor progress: After implementing the changes, it is important to monitor progress to ensure that the improvements are having the desired effect. This can be done by tracking relevant metrics and comparing them to the baseline data.

Make adjustments: Based on the monitoring and evaluation of progress, adjustments may need to be made to the action plan. This could involve refining the objectives, modifying the steps, or reallocating resources to ensure that the improvements continue.

Continuously improve: Finally, addressing areas for improvement based on metrics is an ongoing process. It is important to continuously monitor and evaluate performance, make adjustments as needed, and strive for continuous improvement.

Integration with HR Technology

Integration with HR technology is the process of connecting and synchronizing talent management systems with HR software solutions. This integration enables seamless data flow and communication between different HR systems, resulting in improved efficiency and effectiveness in managing talent.

Integration with HR technology allows Talent specialists to leverage the capabilities of HR software solutions to streamline their talent management processes. It enables them to automate various tasks, gather and analyze data, and make data-driven decisions to attract, develop, and retain top talent.

Here are some key aspects of integration with HR technology in talent management:

1. Applicant Tracking System (ATS) Integration: Integration with an ATS allows Talent specialists to seamlessly transfer applicant data between the ATS and other HR systems. This integration ensures a smooth transition from recruiting to onboarding, enabling a consistent and efficient candidate experience.

2. Performance Management System Integration: Integration with a performance management system enables Talent specialists to align performance objectives with talent development and succession planning. This integration facilitates the tracking of performance data, feedback, and coaching, helping Talent specialists identify high-potential employees and create personalized development plans.

3. Learning Management System (LMS) Integration: Integration with an LMS enables Talent specialists to deliver and track learning and development programs. This integration ensures that employees have access to relevant training materials, enables tracking of training completion and certifications, and supports the identification of skill gaps for targeted development initiatives.

4. Compensation Management System Integration: Integration with a compensation management system allows Talent specialists to automate and streamline the compensation planning and administration process. This integration ensures consistency and fairness in compensation decisions, facilitates reporting and analysis of compensation data, and supports talent retention efforts.

5. HR Analytics Integration: Integration with HR analytics tools provides Talent specialists with valuable insights into talent-related metrics and trends. This integration enables Talent specialists to track key performance indicators, identify areas for improvement, and make data-driven decisions to optimize talent management strategies.

Real-world example:
A Talent specialist at a multinational technology company uses integration with HR technology to streamline their talent acquisition process. They have integrated their ATS with their HRIS (Human Resources Information System) to ensure seamless data flow between the two systems. When a candidate is hired, their data is automatically transferred from the ATS to the HRIS, eliminating the need for manual data entry. This integration saves time, reduces errors, and improves the overall efficiency of the talent acquisition process.

How do you integrate recruitment processes with other HR technologies?

Answer

Integrating recruitment processes with other HR technologies is crucial for efficient talent acquisition. Here are some ways to achieve this integration:
• Applicant Tracking System (ATS): An ATS is a software application that helps manage the recruitment process. It can automate job postings, screen resumes, schedule interviews, and track candidate progress. Integrating the ATS with other HR technologies allows for seamless data flow and reduces manual effort. For example, when a candidate is hired, the ATS can automatically update the HRIS (Human Resource Information System) and payroll system.
• HRIS (Human Resource Information System): An HRIS is a central database that stores employee information, such as personal details, job history, and performance evaluations. Integrating the recruitment process with the HRIS ensures that candidate data is easily accessible and can be used for future talent management. For

instance, if a candidate is not selected for a particular position, their information can be stored in the HRIS for future reference when a suitable opportunity arises.

• Video Interviewing Platforms: With the rise of remote work, video interviewing platforms have become essential for conducting virtual interviews. Integrating these platforms with recruitment processes allows for streamlined scheduling, recording, and evaluation of video interviews. This integration can save time and eliminate the need for in-person interviews, especially in global talent acquisition.

• Onboarding Software: Onboarding software helps new hires transition smoothly into their roles by providing them with necessary information, training materials, and paperwork. Integrating recruitment processes with onboarding software ensures a seamless transition from the candidate stage to the employee stage. For example, once a candidate accepts a job offer, their information can be automatically transferred to the onboarding software, triggering the onboarding process.

By integrating recruitment processes with other HR technologies, organizations can optimize their talent acquisition efforts and improve the overall candidate experience.

Discuss your experience with implementing or optimizing an ATS?

Answer

In my role as a Talent Acquisition Specialist specializing in top-tier IT companies, I have extensive experience in implementing and optimizing Applicant Tracking Systems (ATS). Here are some highlights of my experience:

Implemented an ATS for a leading tech company with over 500 employees. This involved working closely with the HR team to understand their specific recruitment needs and configuring the system accordingly. I conducted thorough research to identify the best ATS solution for their requirements and managed the entire implementation process from start to finish. This included data migration, system customization, and training sessions for HR staff to ensure they were comfortable using the new system.

Optimized an existing ATS for a rapidly growing startup. The company had been using an ATS for a while but was facing issues with efficiency and scalability. I conducted a comprehensive audit of the system and identified areas for improvement. Based on my findings, I recommended and implemented changes such as streamlining workflows, automating manual processes, and integrating the ATS with other HR systems. These optimizations significantly improved the recruitment process, resulting in faster time-to-hire and better candidate experiences.

Utilized data analytics to continuously improve ATS performance. I leveraged the reporting and analytics capabilities of the ATS to track key recruitment metrics such as time-to-fill, cost-per-hire, and source effectiveness. By analyzing this data, I was able to identify bottlenecks in the recruitment process, make data-driven decisions, and implement targeted improvements to enhance the overall efficiency and effectiveness of the ATS.

Regularly stay updated with the latest industry trends and best practices in ATS implementation and optimization. I actively participate in webinars, attend conferences, and engage with professional networks to stay abreast of the evolving landscape of recruitment technology. This allows me to bring innovative ideas and cutting-edge solutions to my work as a Talent Acquisition Specialist.

What role does automation play in your recruitment strategy?

Answer

Automation plays a crucial role in our recruitment strategy as a Talent Acquisition Specialist specializing in top-tier IT companies. It helps streamline the hiring process and improves efficiency. Here are some key ways automation is used in our recruitment strategy:

• Resume screening: Automation tools are used to quickly scan and filter through a large number of resumes, saving time and effort. These tools can identify keywords, skills, and experience that match the job requirements, allowing us to shortlist the most relevant candidates for further evaluation.

• Candidate sourcing: Automation is used to search and identify potential candidates from various online platforms, professional networks, and databases. This helps us expand our talent pool and reach a wider audience.

• Application tracking: Automation tools are used to track and manage candidate applications throughout the recruitment process. This includes sending automated notifications and updates to candidates, scheduling interviews, and managing feedback from hiring managers.

• Interview scheduling: Automation tools can help streamline the interview scheduling process by automatically coordinating availability between candidates and interviewers. This reduces the back-and-forth communication and ensures a smooth scheduling experience for all parties involved.

• Candidate assessment: Automation is used to administer and score online assessments, tests, and coding challenges. This helps evaluate candidates' technical skills and abilities objectively and consistently.

• Onboarding: Automation tools can be used to automate the onboarding process for new hires, including generating offer letters, collecting necessary documents, and providing access to relevant systems and resources.

These are just a few examples of how automation plays a role in our recruitment strategy. By leveraging automation, we can save time, improve efficiency, and focus on the most important aspect of recruitment – finding the best talent for our top-tier IT companies.

How do you ensure data accuracy and integrity in recruitment technology?

Answer
Implement data validation checks to ensure the accuracy of the data entered into the system. This can include verifying the format, consistency, and completeness of the data. For example, requiring certain fields to be filled out before a candidate can be added to the system.

Regularly update and maintain the database to ensure that outdated or inaccurate data is removed or corrected. This can involve conducting data audits, cleaning up duplicate records, and verifying the accuracy of contact information. For example, regularly reviewing and updating candidate profiles to ensure that their current employment status and contact information is up to date.

Implement security measures to protect the integrity of the data. This can include restricting access to sensitive information, implementing secure login processes, and regularly backing up data to prevent loss or corruption. For example, using role-based access control to limit access to certain recruitment data to only authorized personnel.

Train recruiters and hiring managers on the importance of data accuracy and integrity, as well as the proper use of the recruitment technology. This can involve providing training on data entry best practices, system usage guidelines, and security protocols. For example, conducting regular training sessions on how to properly enter and update candidate information in the recruitment system.

Monitor and analyze data quality metrics to identify any issues or trends that may indicate data inaccuracies or integrity issues. This can involve tracking metrics such as data completeness, accuracy, timeliness, and consistency. For example, regularly reviewing data quality reports to identify areas for improvement and taking corrective actions.

Summary: To ensure data accuracy and integrity in recruitment technology, it is important to implement data validation checks, regularly update and maintain the database, implement security measures, train recruiters and hiring managers, and monitor data quality metrics. By following these steps, recruitment technology can be used effectively to support talent acquisition processes.

www.ingramcontent.com/pod-product-compliance
Lightning Source LLC
Chambersburg PA
CBHW050449290526
45786CB00006B/2226